Sacred Spaces
& Special Places

Navigating the Blue Ridge

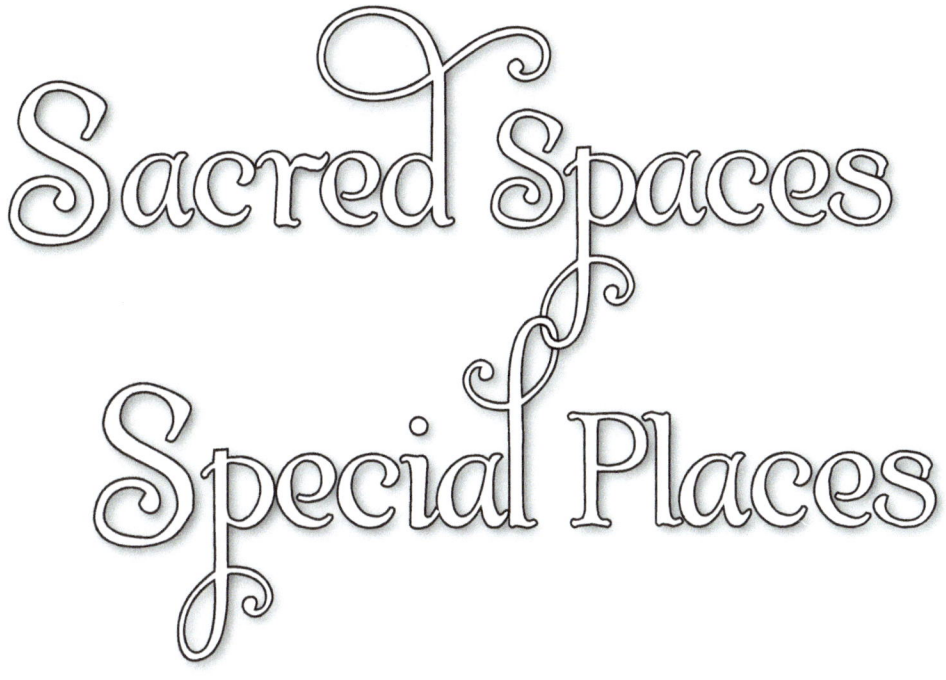

Sacred Spaces Special Places

Navigating the Blue Ridge

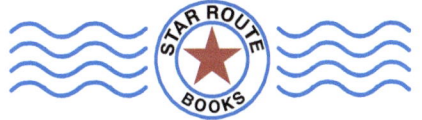

STAR ROUTE BOOKS
SPARTA ★ NORTH CAROLINA

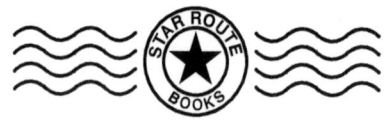

an imprint of Imaging Specialists, Inc.

Sacred Spaces
Special Places
Navigating the Blue Ridge

ISBN 978-0-9882647-3-1

First printing, June 2013

WWW.STARROUTEBOOKS.COM

Contents

Preface

Our original idea for this second photo collection was to make it about churches in the area. But there are a lot of churches in the area. To include them all would be difficult, and we'd probably get nasty comments from those we would, inevitably, leave out. Nasty people always comment, but they're the very ones I'd leave out.

So these are some of our favorite places. It is only a coincidence that many are churches. Many are courthouses or barns. Sometimes, the most sacred places include no sign of the hand of man and sometimes, the most secular scene proves the work of God.

When I look at a photograph, even my own, I almost always ask myself, "Is this man's doing or the Lord's?" or in other words, is it a good photograph because of the eye or the skill of the photographer or because it was a beautiful scene that any six year-old could have snapped?

A photograph is only a viewpoint- or a recording of what we have seen when we saw it and how we saw it. So the answer has to be, that, the photographer is responsible for the shot. The photographer chose the optimal time and place using training, skills and talent God gave them to record what God showed them.

1 Corinthians 13:12 says, "For now we see through a glass, darkly," and though I don't want to preach, I do want to suggest that, at our best, we can see and record only a fraction of what is there. And my (or anyone's) perception of beauty or fine art, is limited to the light God shows each of us.

With that in mind, some of the images included here were well thought out and some I couldn't even articulate why I like them, but I do. And I hope you do, too.

Jeff Halsey
May, 2013

1. **Coxs Chapel** United Methodist Church just before an early spring squall.

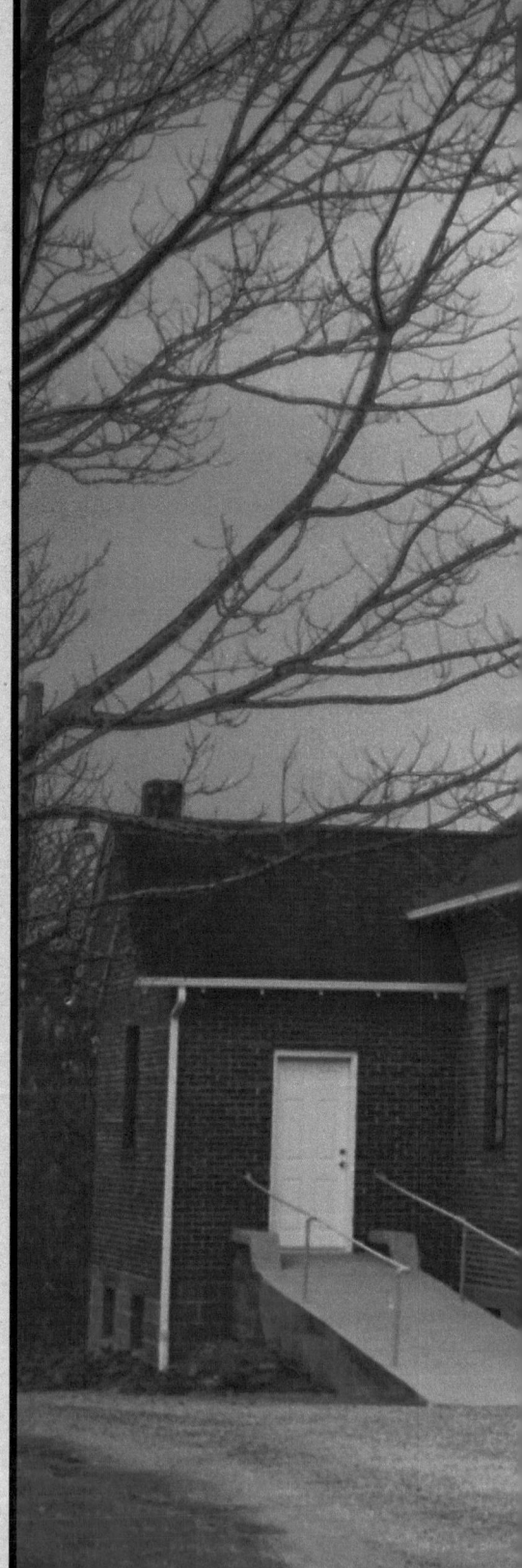

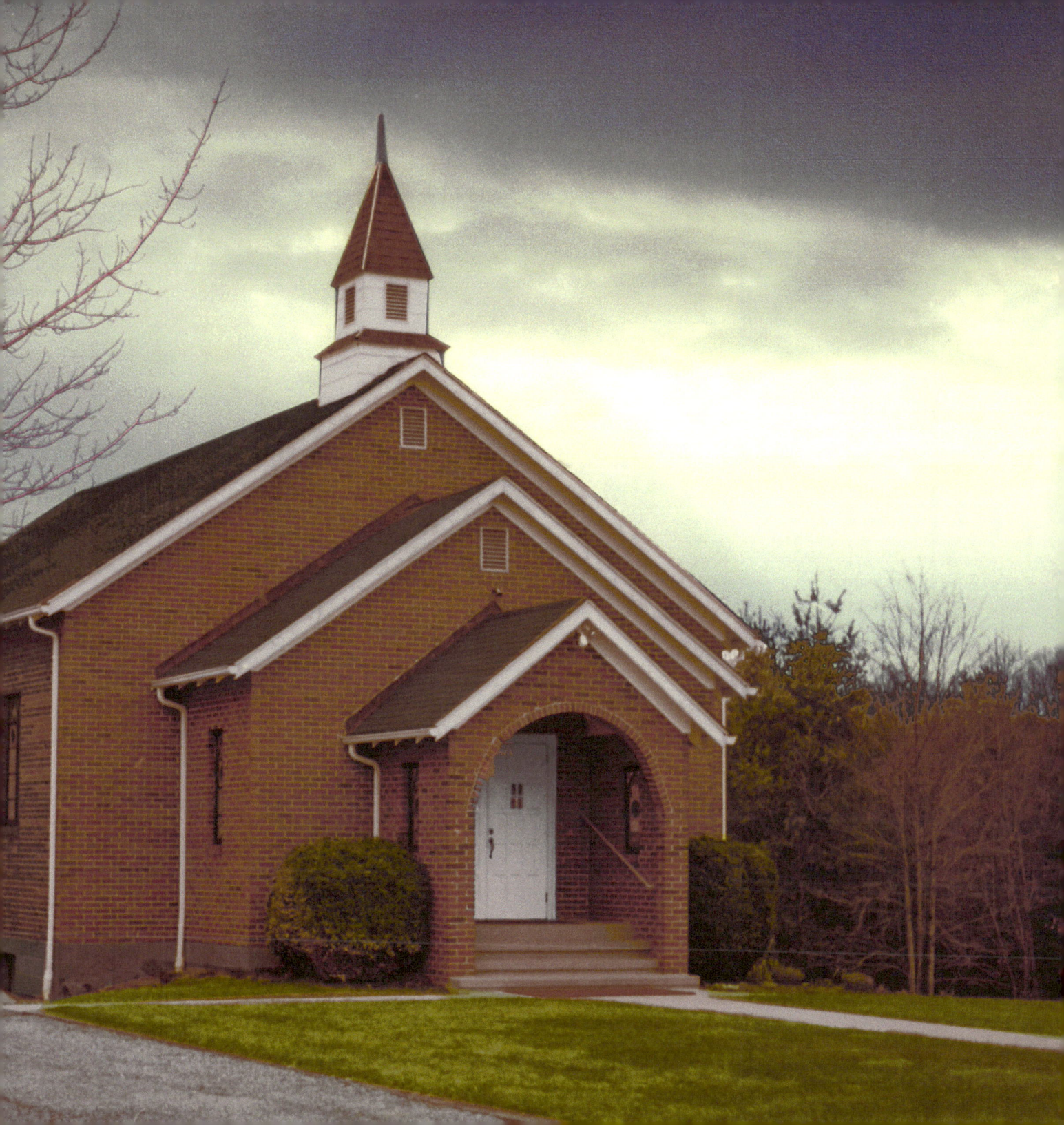

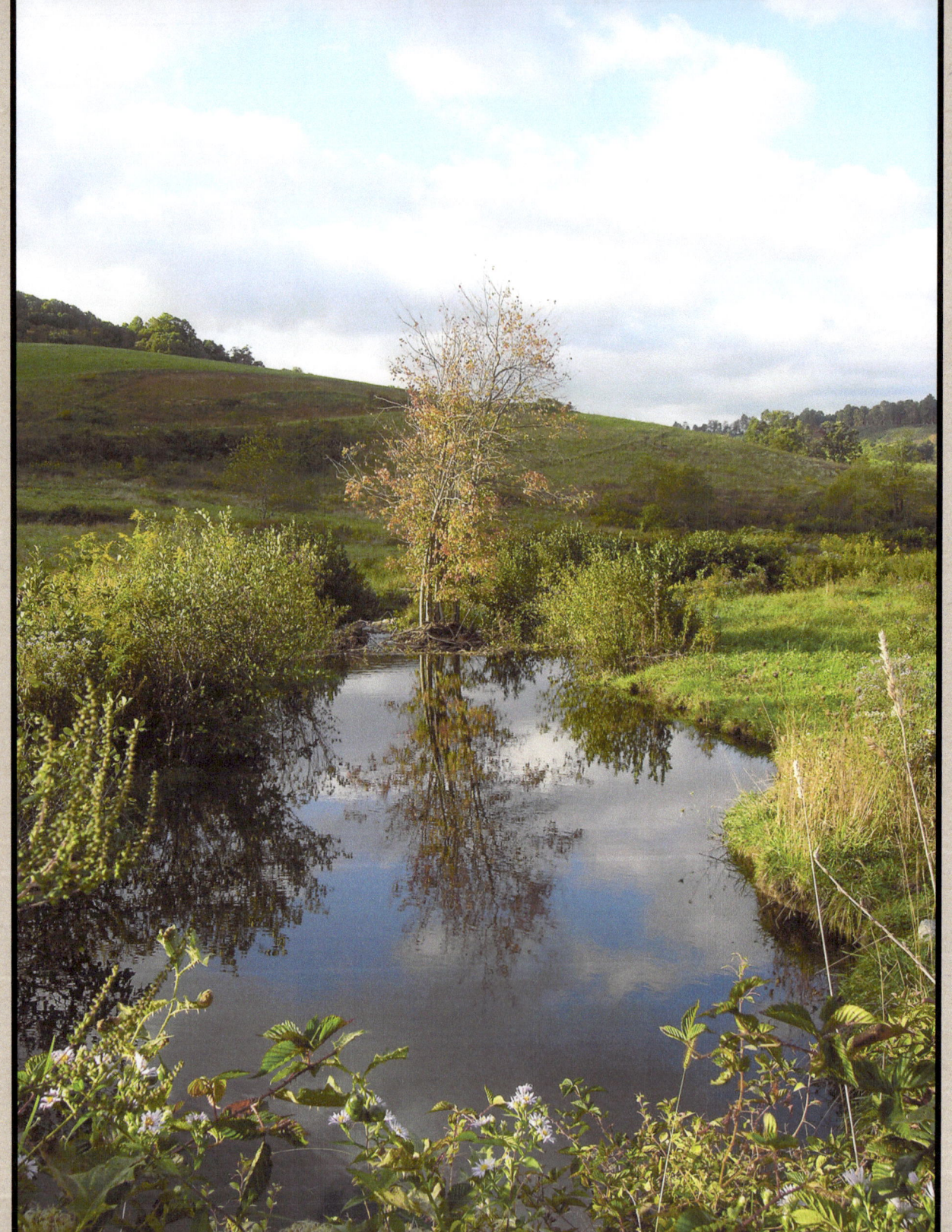

2. **New Dam** on Prathers Creek. The beavers were forcibly evicted from their last home and chose to relocate, here.

3. **Potato Creek Church.**
GPS Coordinates: Go to
Mouth of Wilson and ask.

4. **Playing Court.**
The Alleghany Community
Theater presentation of
Inherit the Wind, a play about
the controversial "Scopes
Monkey Trial."
Not a soul, afterward, came
forward to join the monkey camp.
(Following pages)

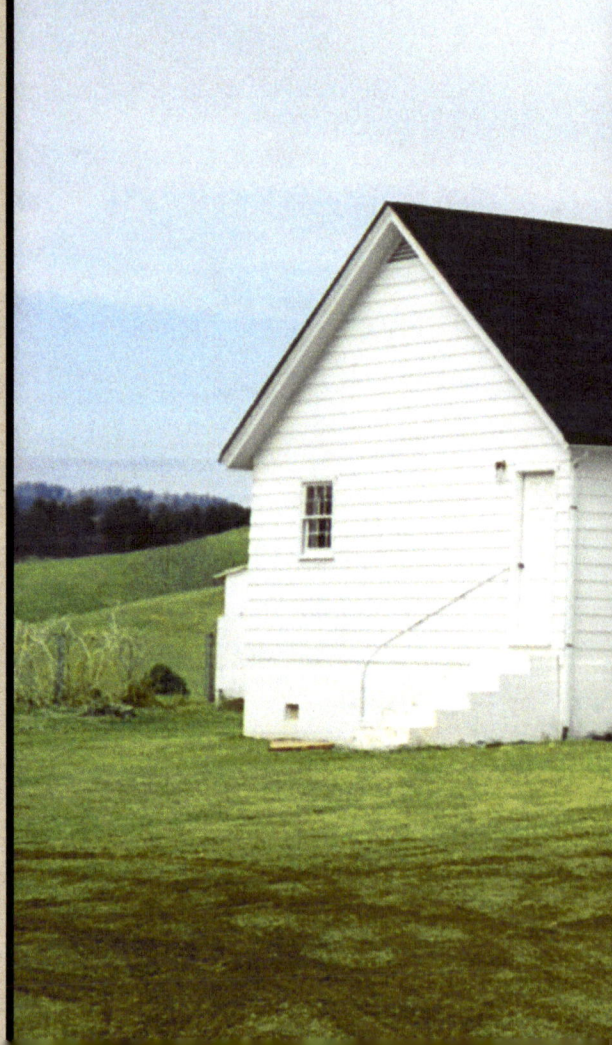

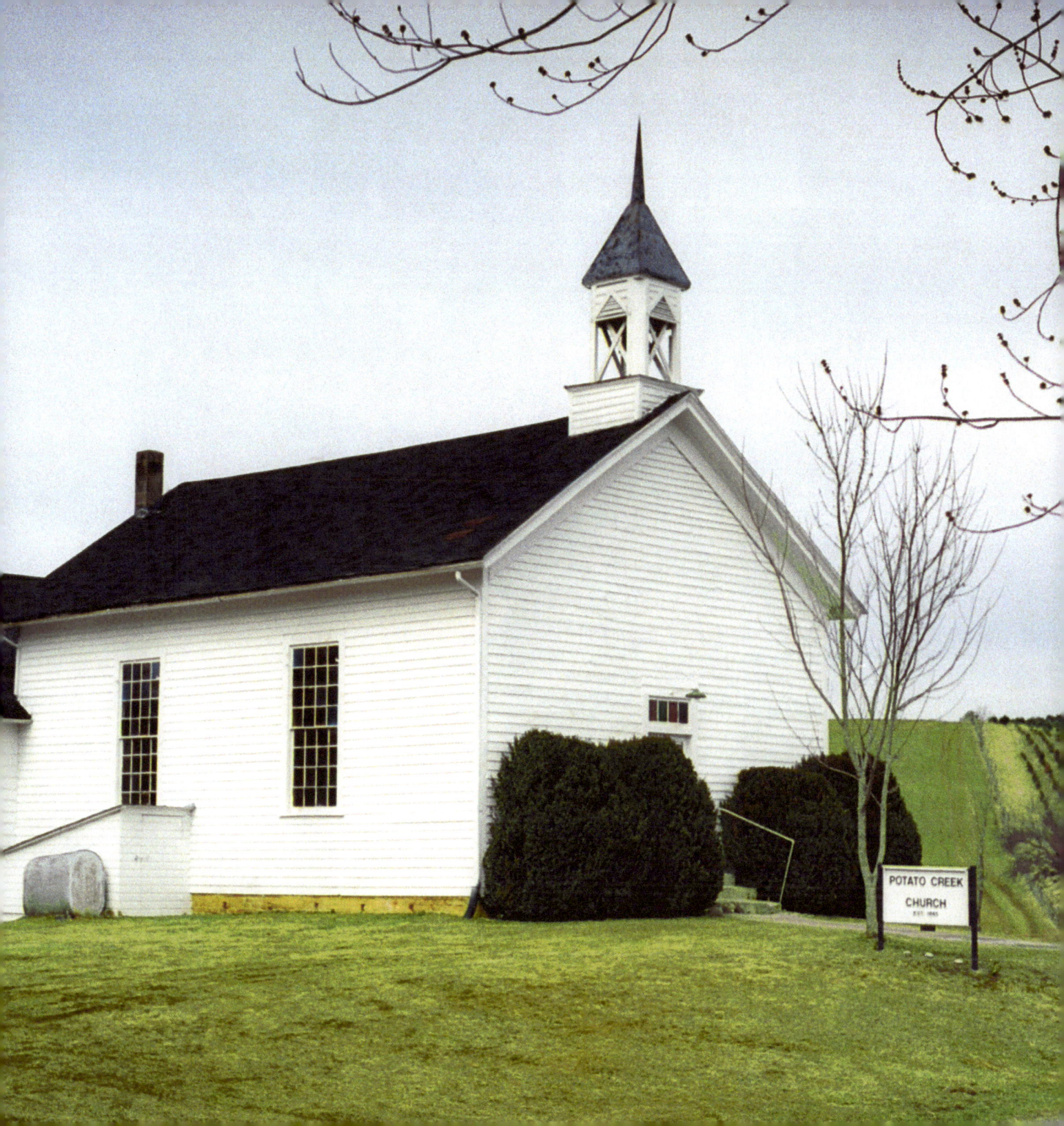

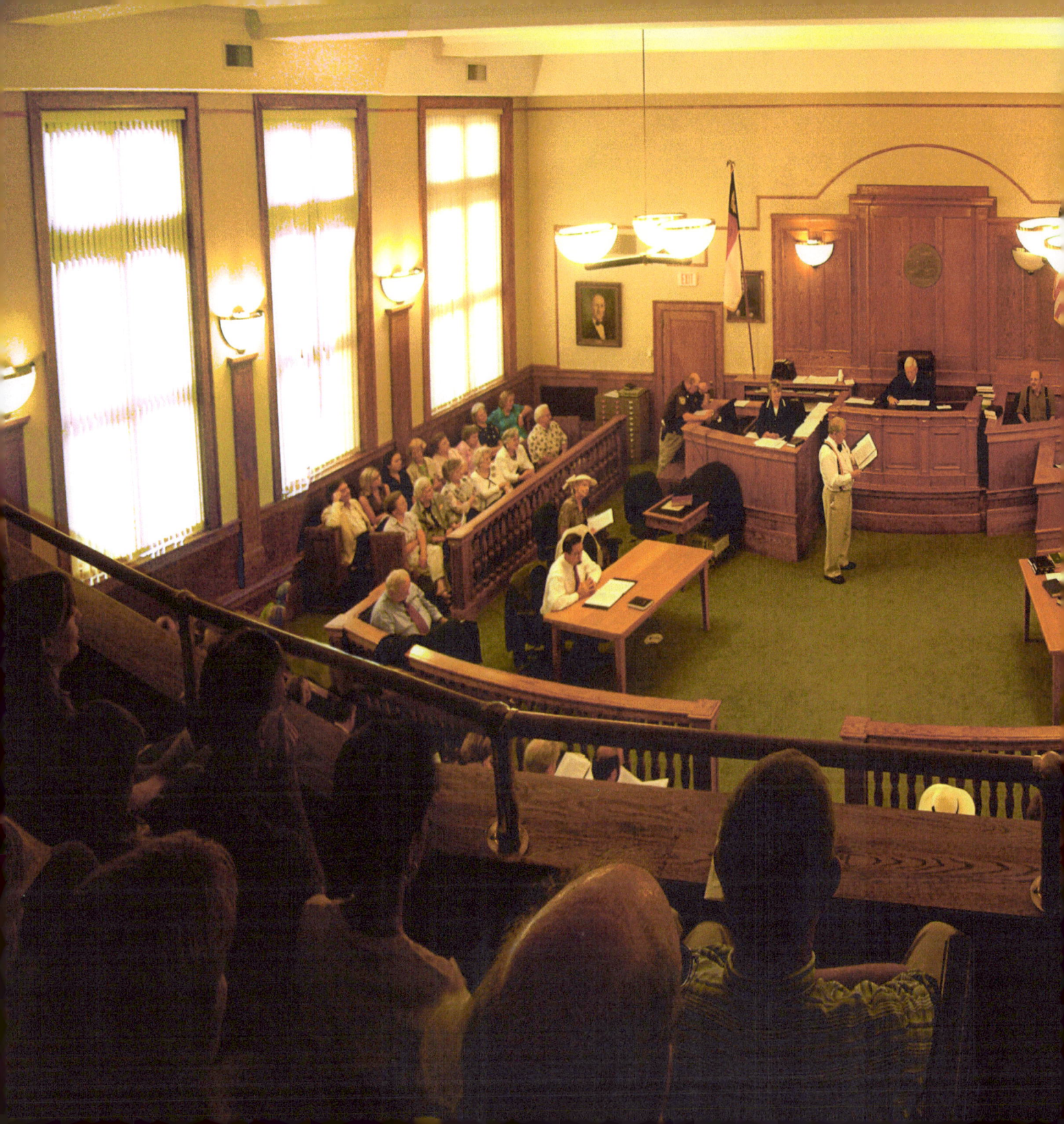

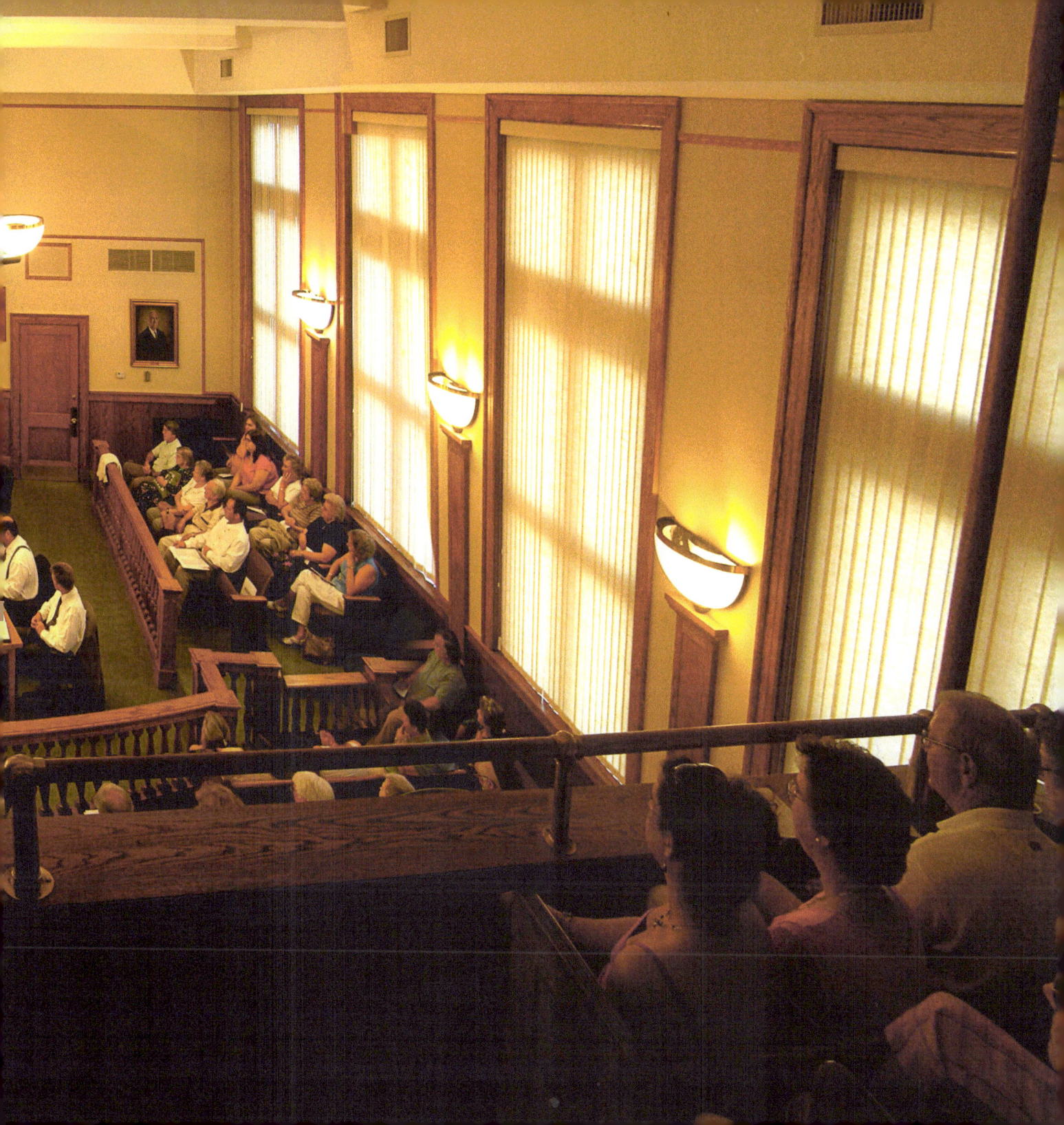

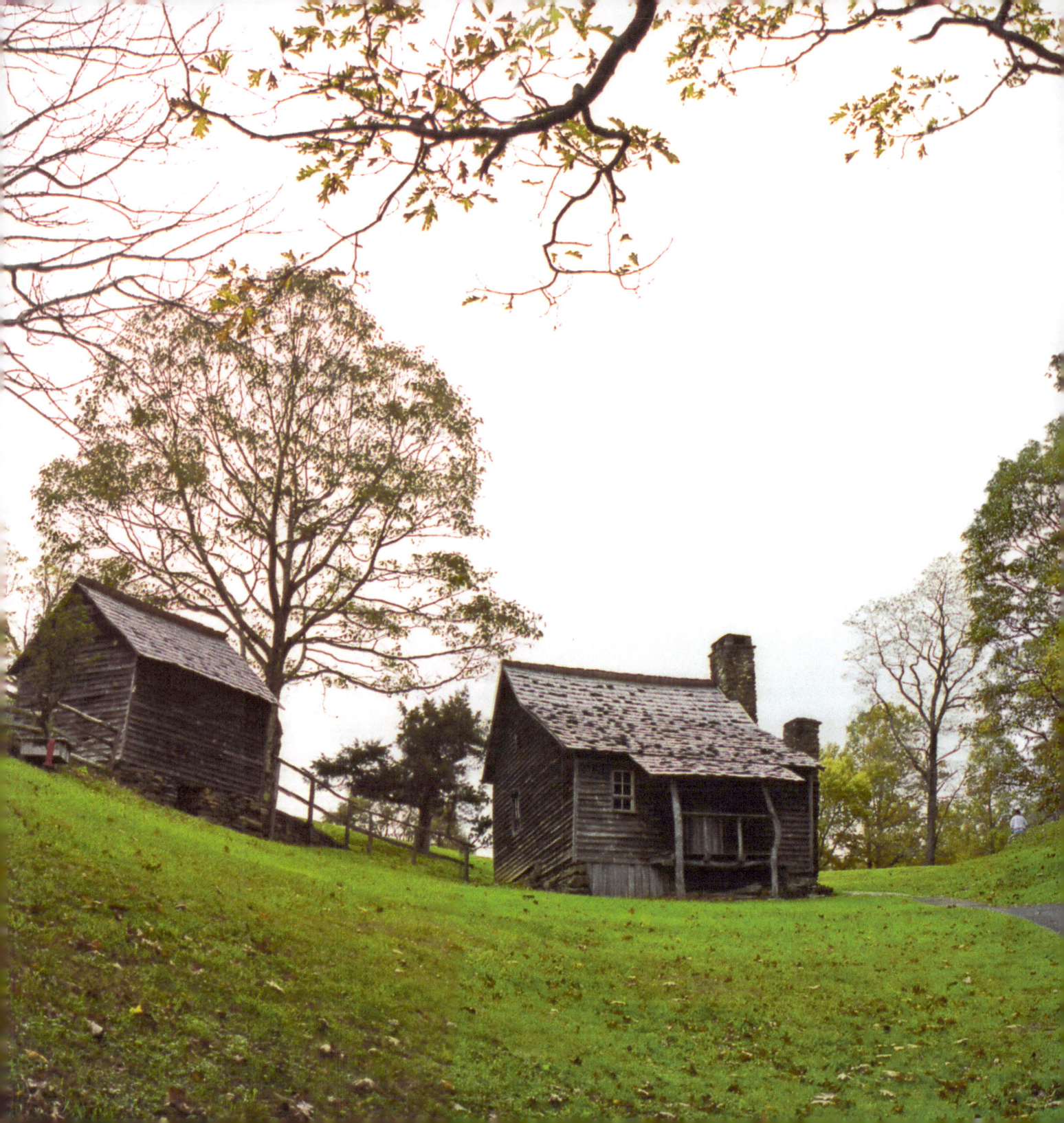

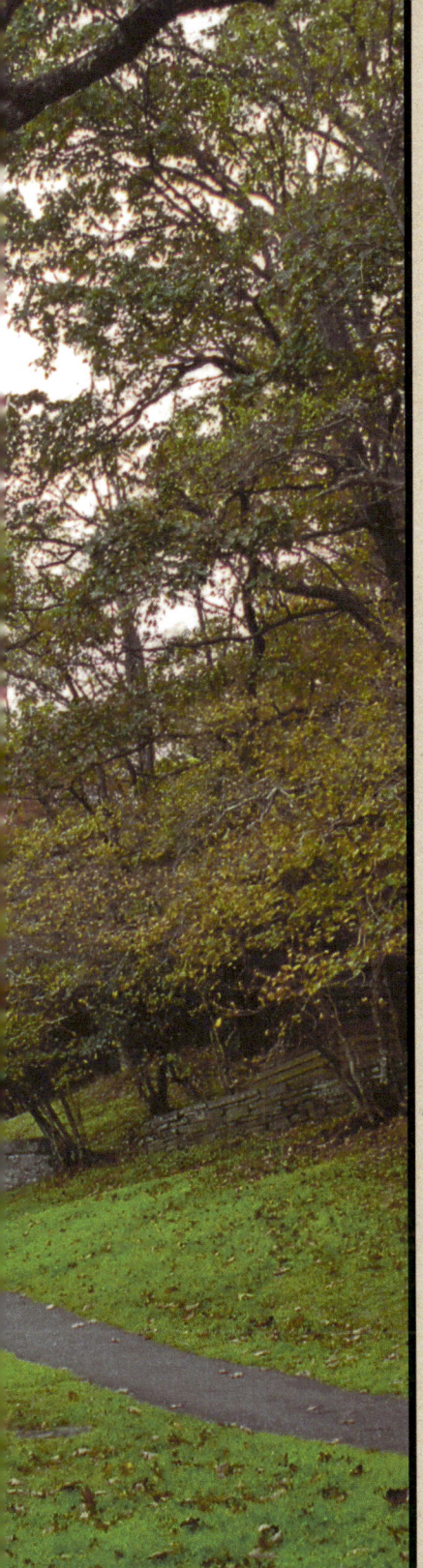

5. **Brinegar's Cabin**.
On the crest of the Blue Ridge before the crest of the Blue Ridge was cool.

Mr. Brinegar's obituary, written by his son John Brinegar:

"Brother Martin Brinegar was born December 11, 1856, and died April 25, 1925, making his stay on earth 68 years, 4 months and four days. He was married to Caroline Joines about 48 years ago. Unto this union were born 4 children, 2 living and 2 dead. He professed a hope in Christ and joined the church at Pleasant Grove about 36 years ago.

"He was taken with pneumonia and lived 8 days. He leaves a wife and 2 children and 4 grandchildren to mourn their loss. He was loved by all who knew him.

"*Fair well wife and children dear,*
No more I'll lead you while you stay here.
For me do not weep, lament or sigh,
But meet in the sweet bye and bye."

6. **Independence Courthouse.**
   Built in 1908, and governing Grayson
   County in stately silence until its
   retirement in 1999.

7. **Green, Gray and Gold.**
   The morning sun at Bullhead Mountain.
   This shot was made after a friend advised
   me to "get your camera and your behind
      there. Now!"
   (Following pages)

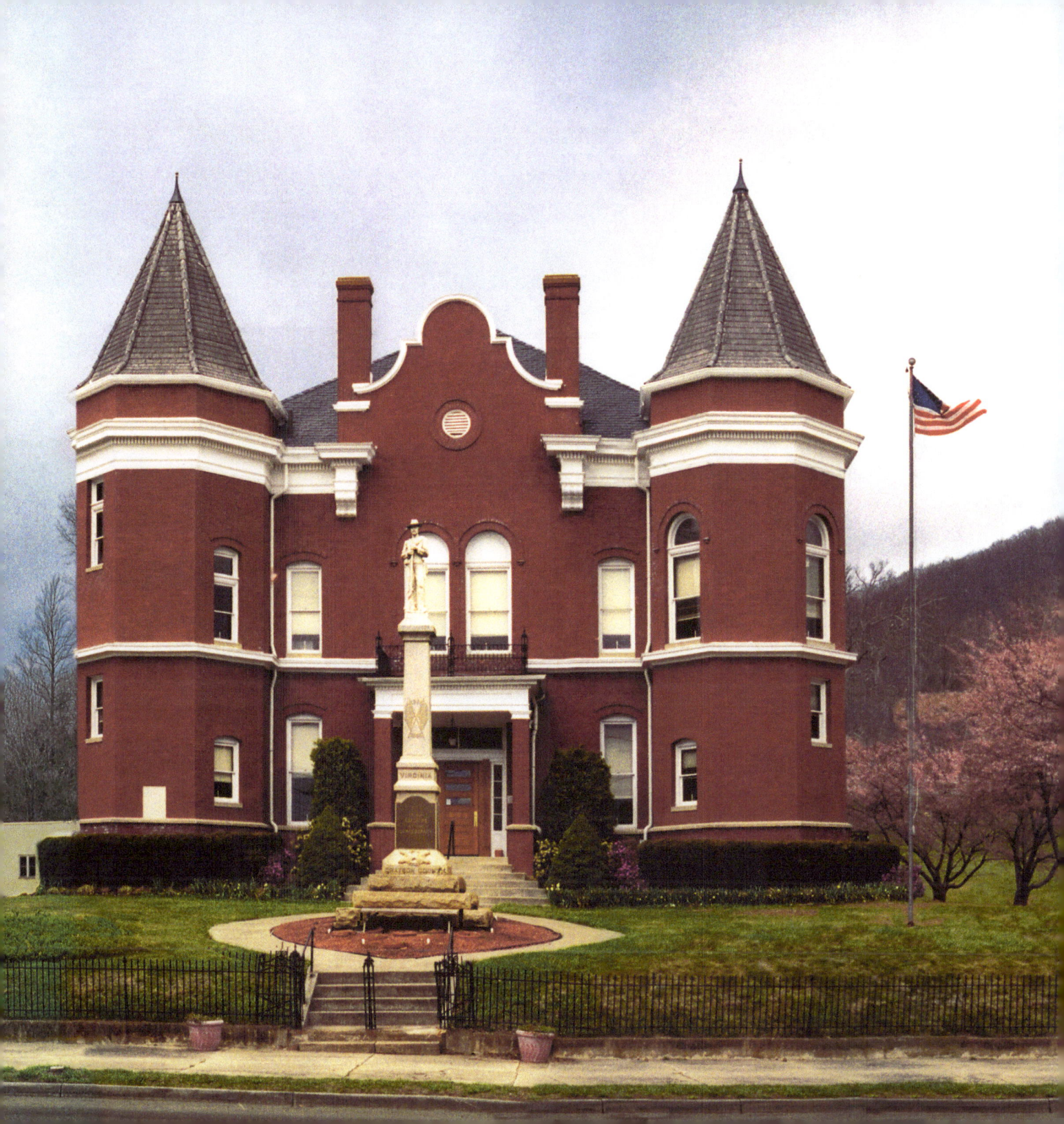

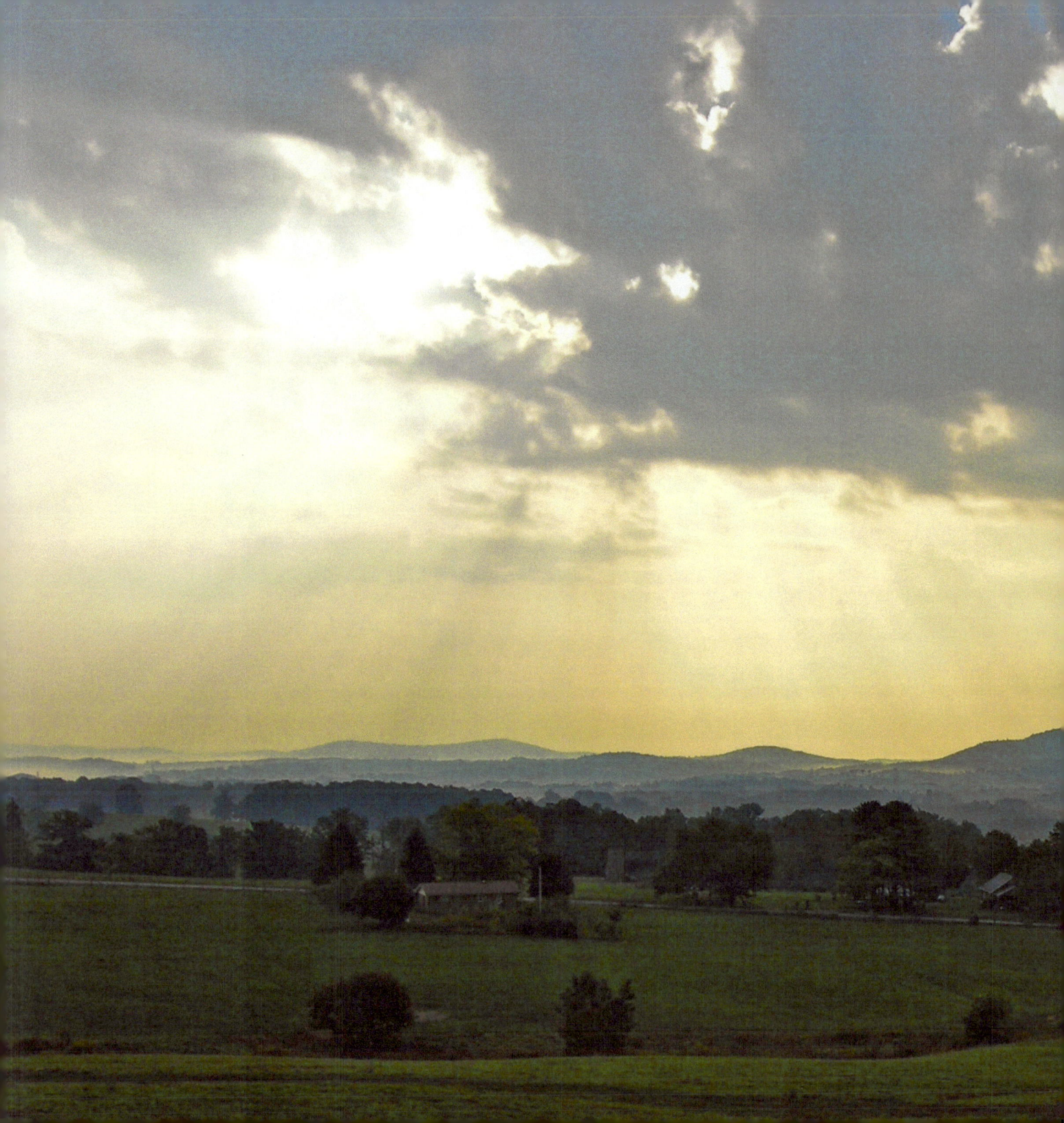

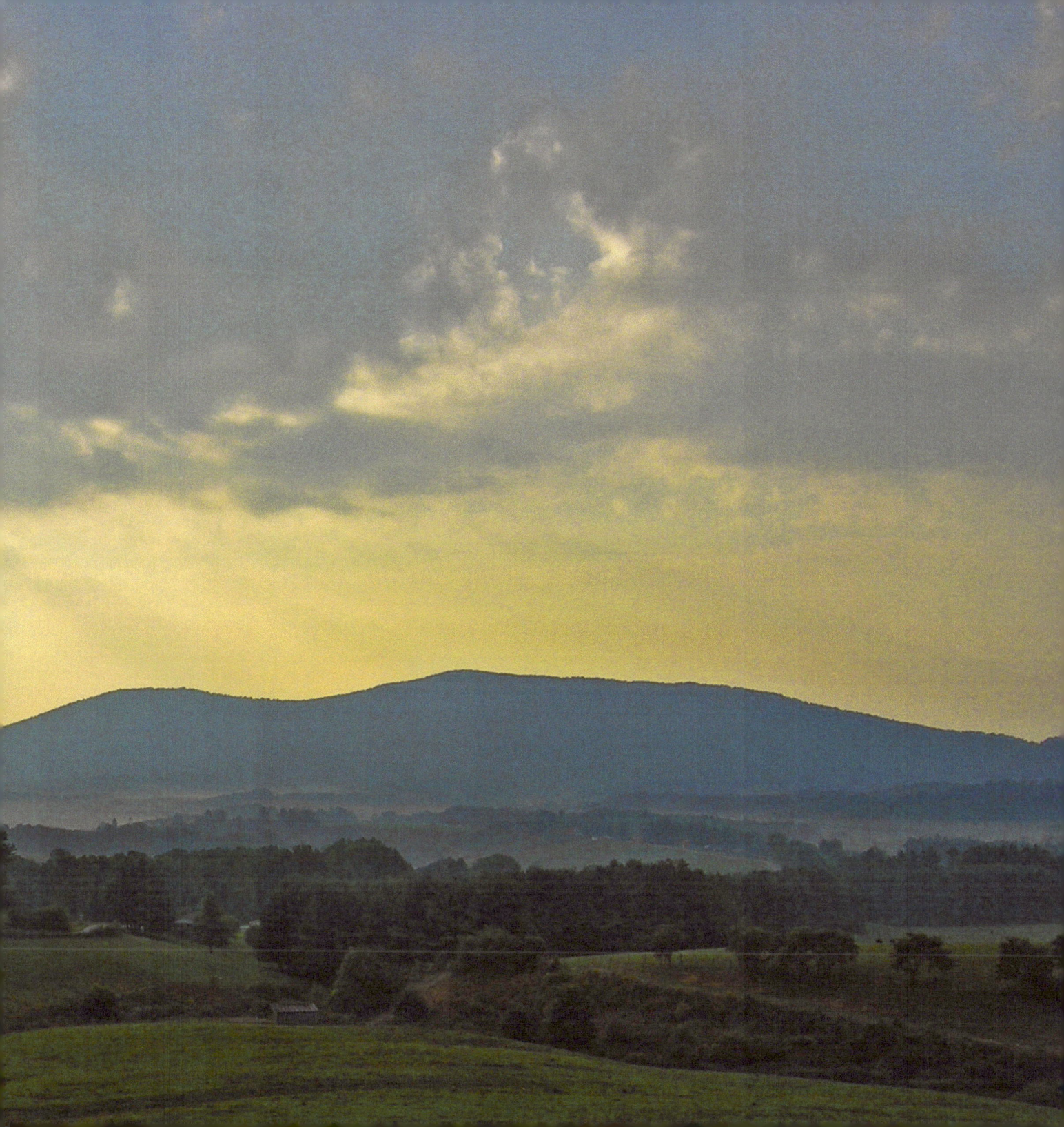

8. **Grassy Creek United Methodist Church.**
From 2004, shot for the Centennial at Grassy Creek.
If you've never visited, you should.
It's a beautiful old building- as nice inside as outside-
and the folks are friendly, too.

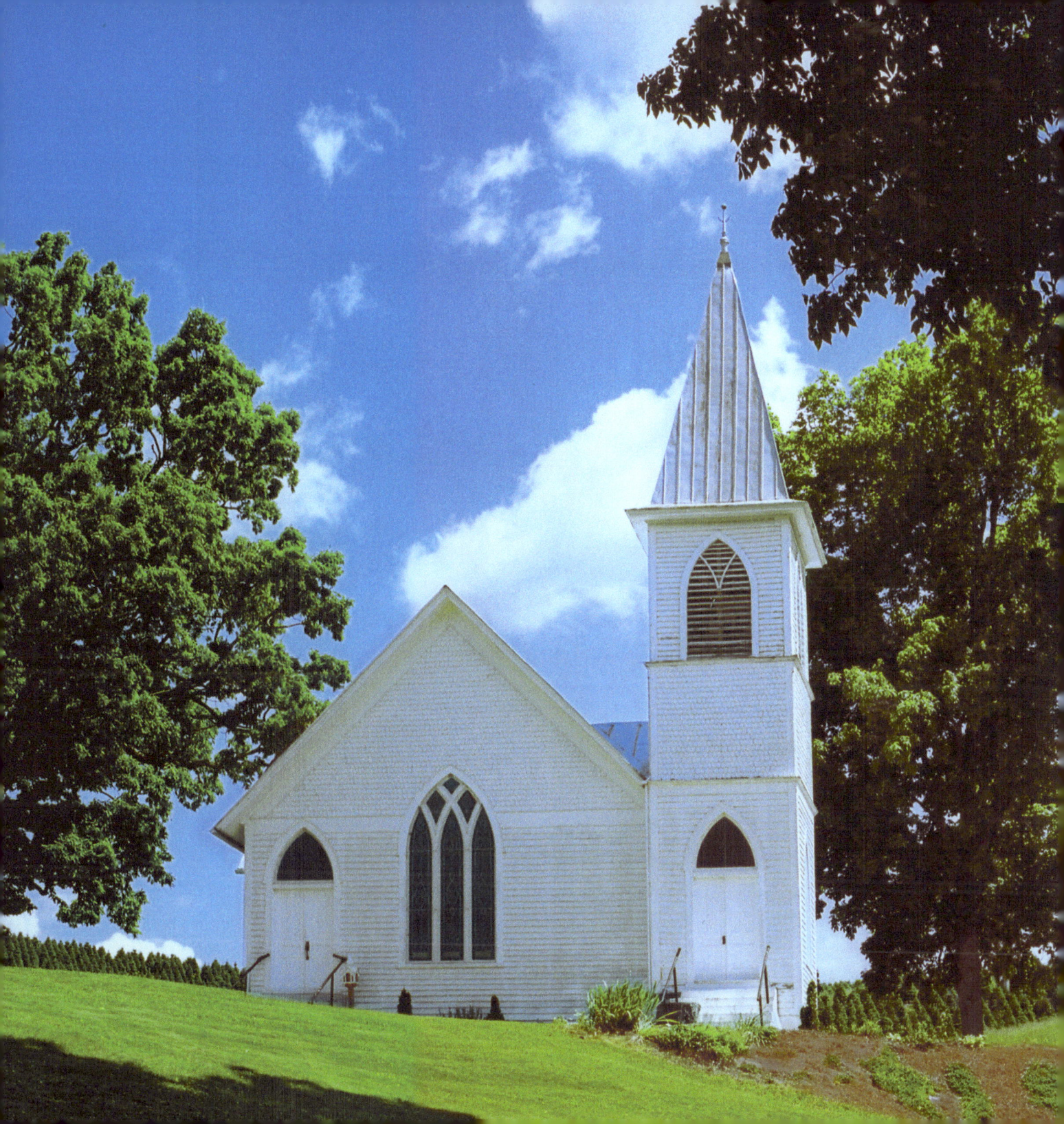

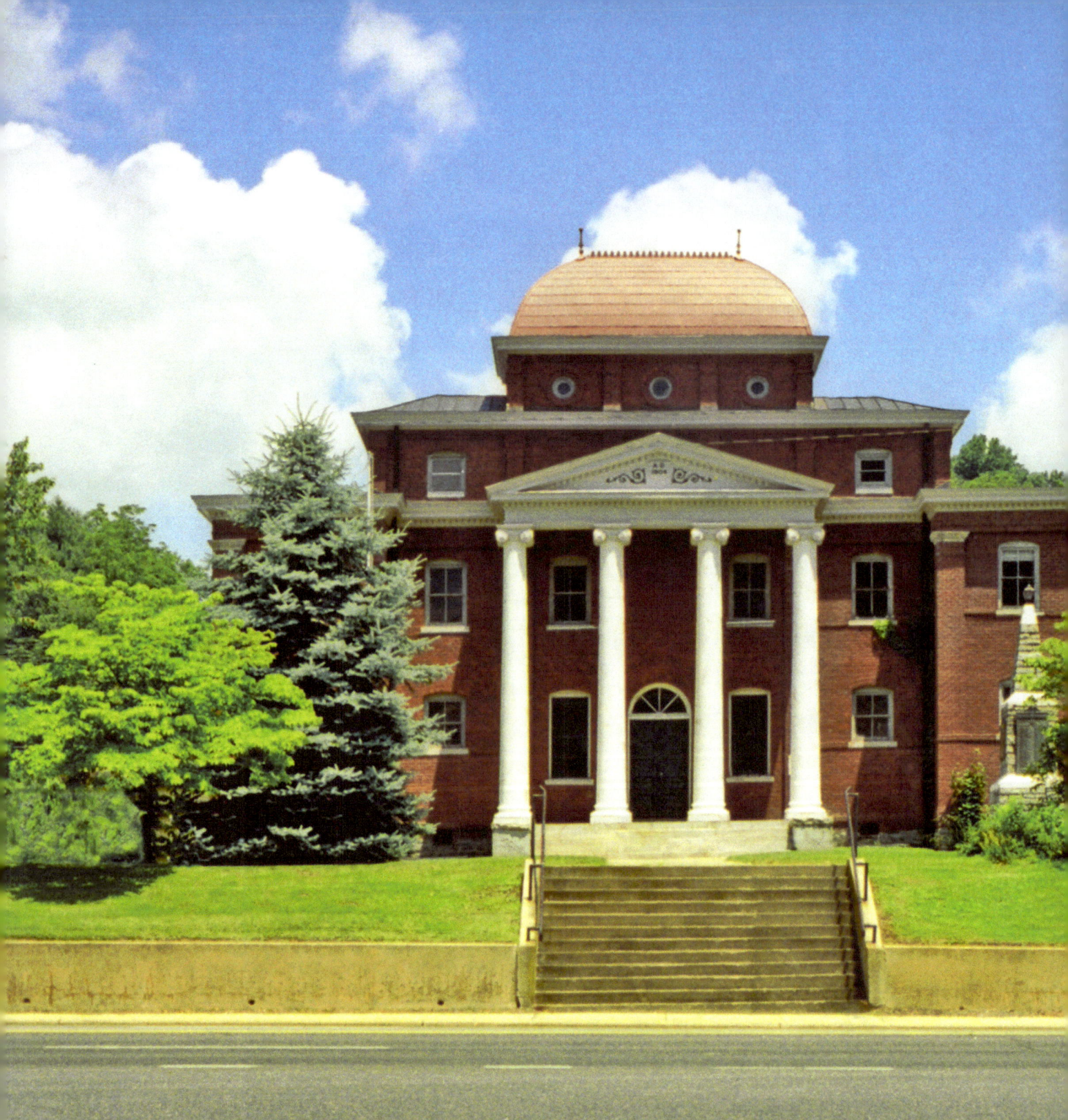

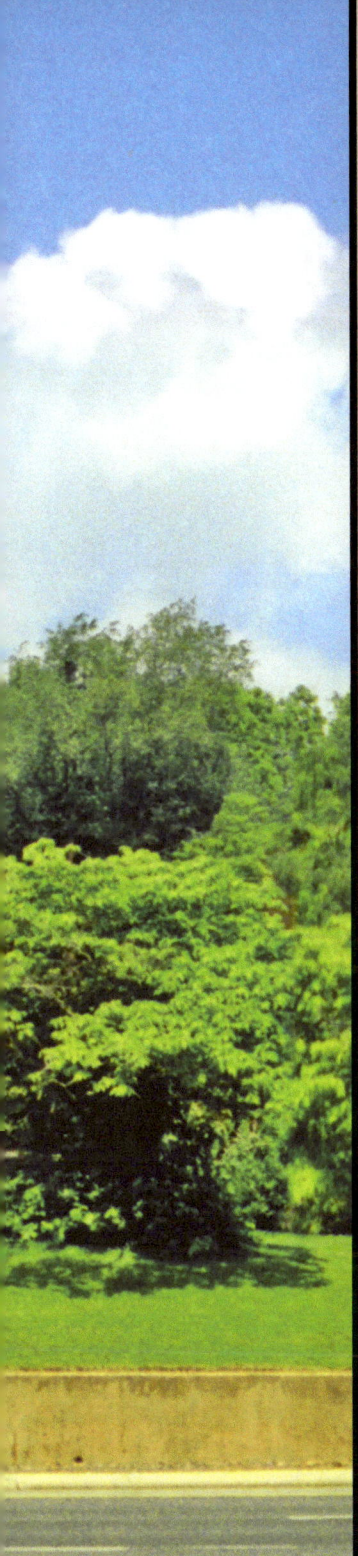

9. **Old Jefferson Courthouse.**
Now the Museum of Ashe County History, it's being restored inside, down to the original paint colors and fireplace mantels.

Perfectly re-purposed, it's as if they held court for decades in the future museum.

10. **View at Flat Top Manor**.
The comfortable and beautiful mountain retreat of an old and venerable, typical Southern family.
(Following pages)

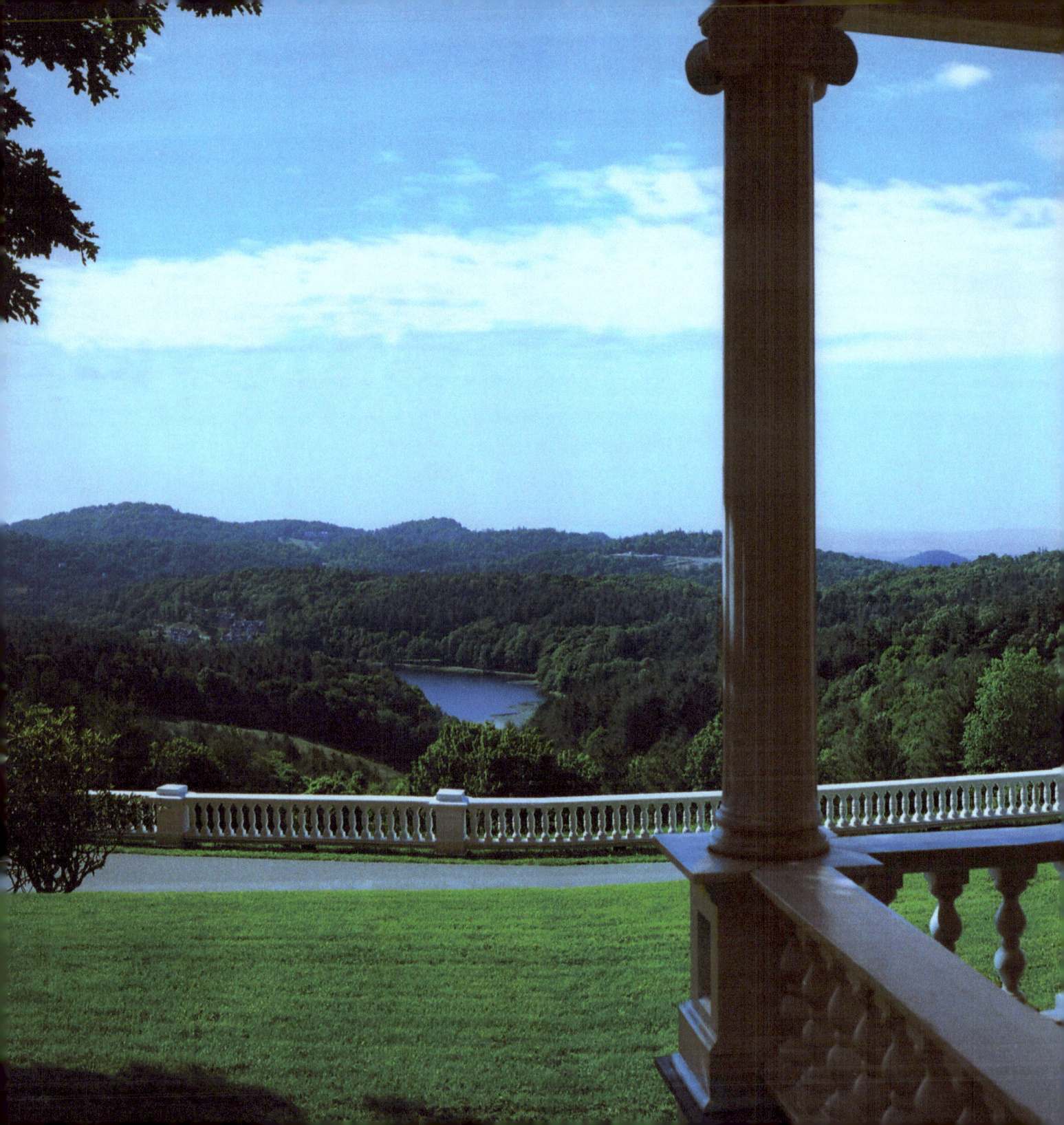

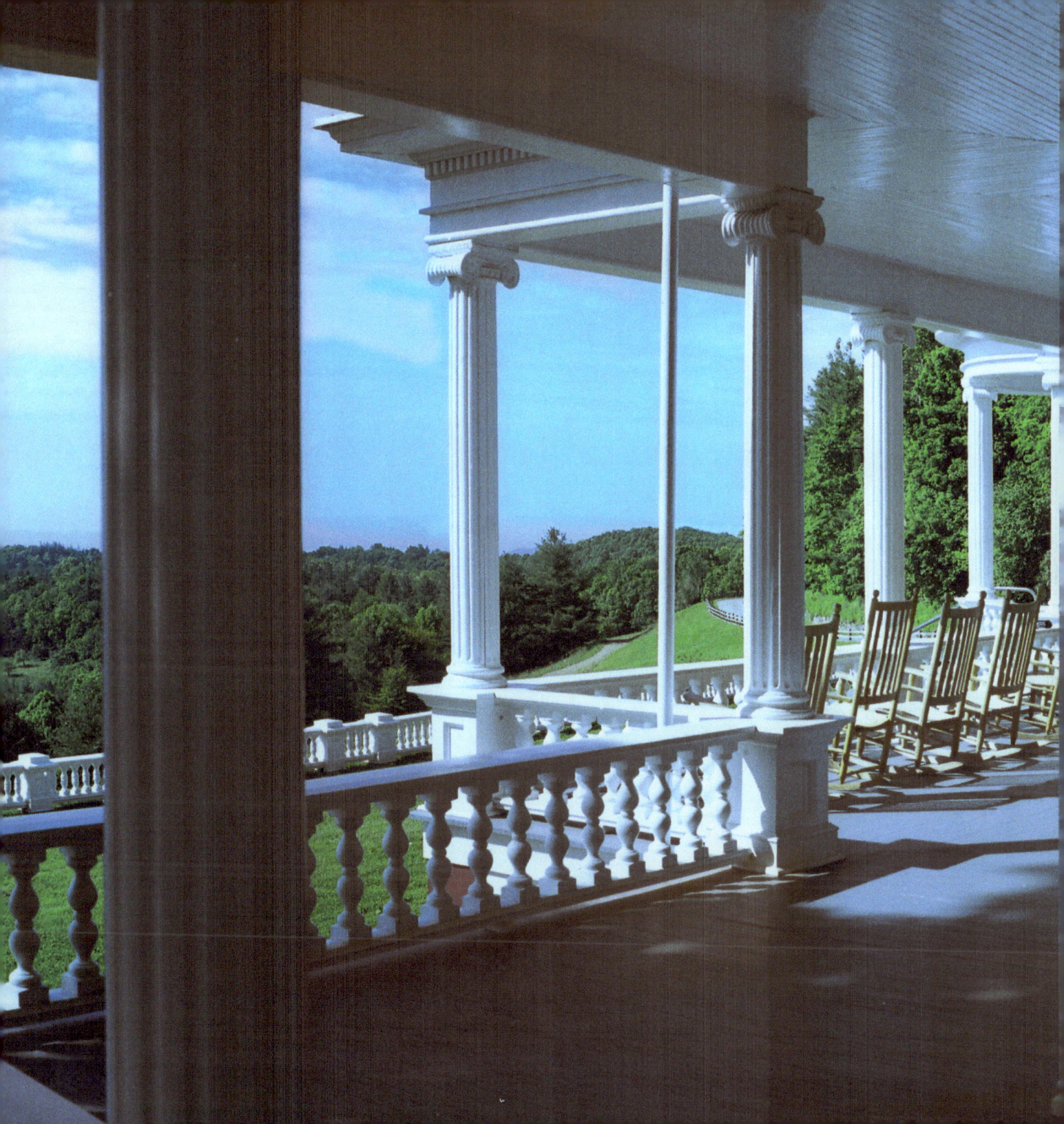

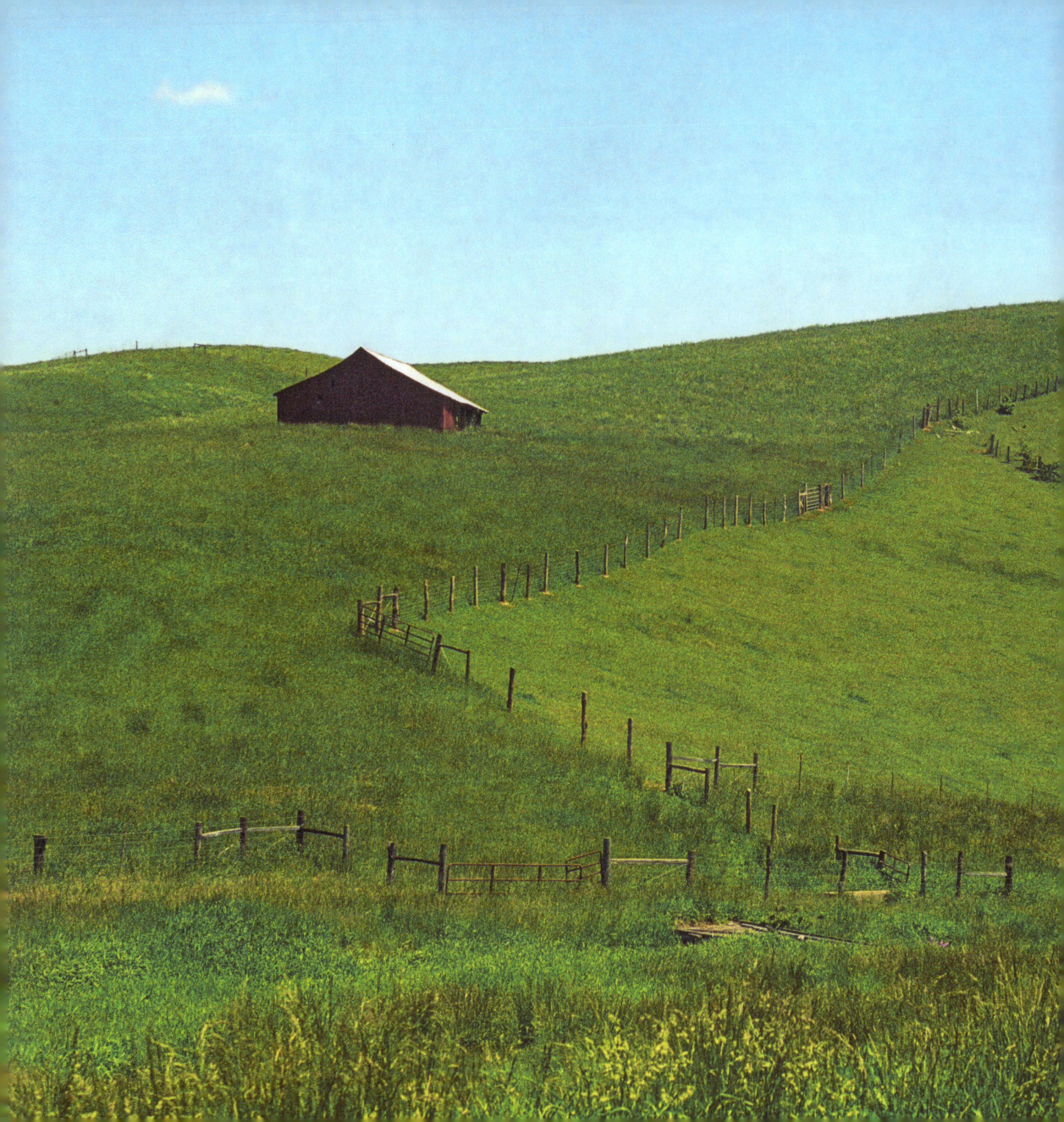

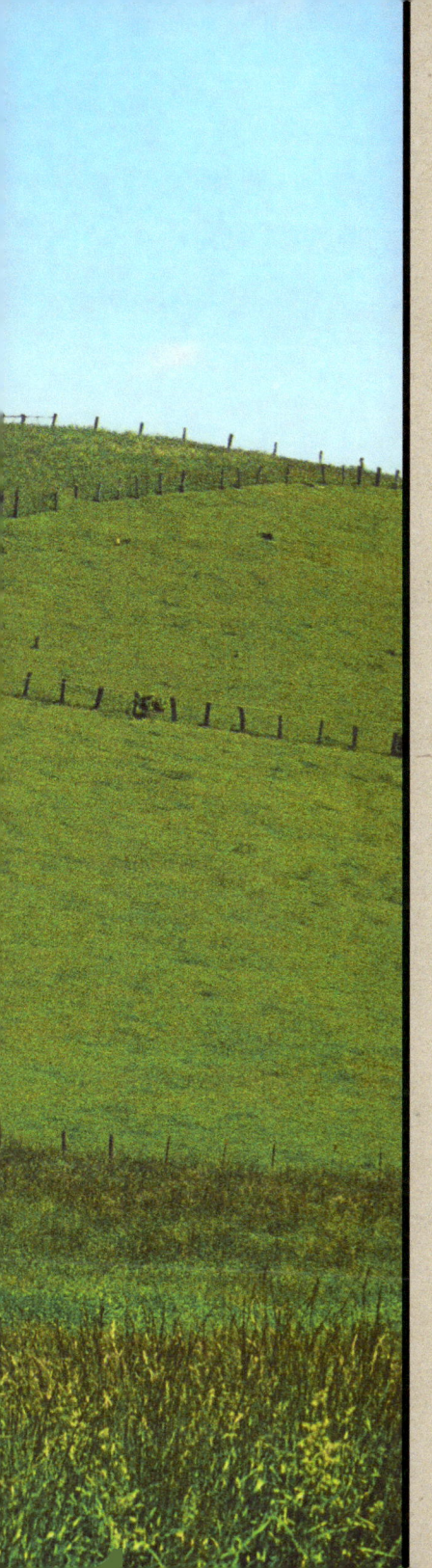

11. **Glenn's Barn**.
These hills are across the road from Glenn & family's *Halsey Farm Supply* in Mouth of Wilson, Virginia, and have been there as long as I can remember.

12. **Downtown Piney Creek, NC**.
   Not really, but it ain't far. You can walk it.

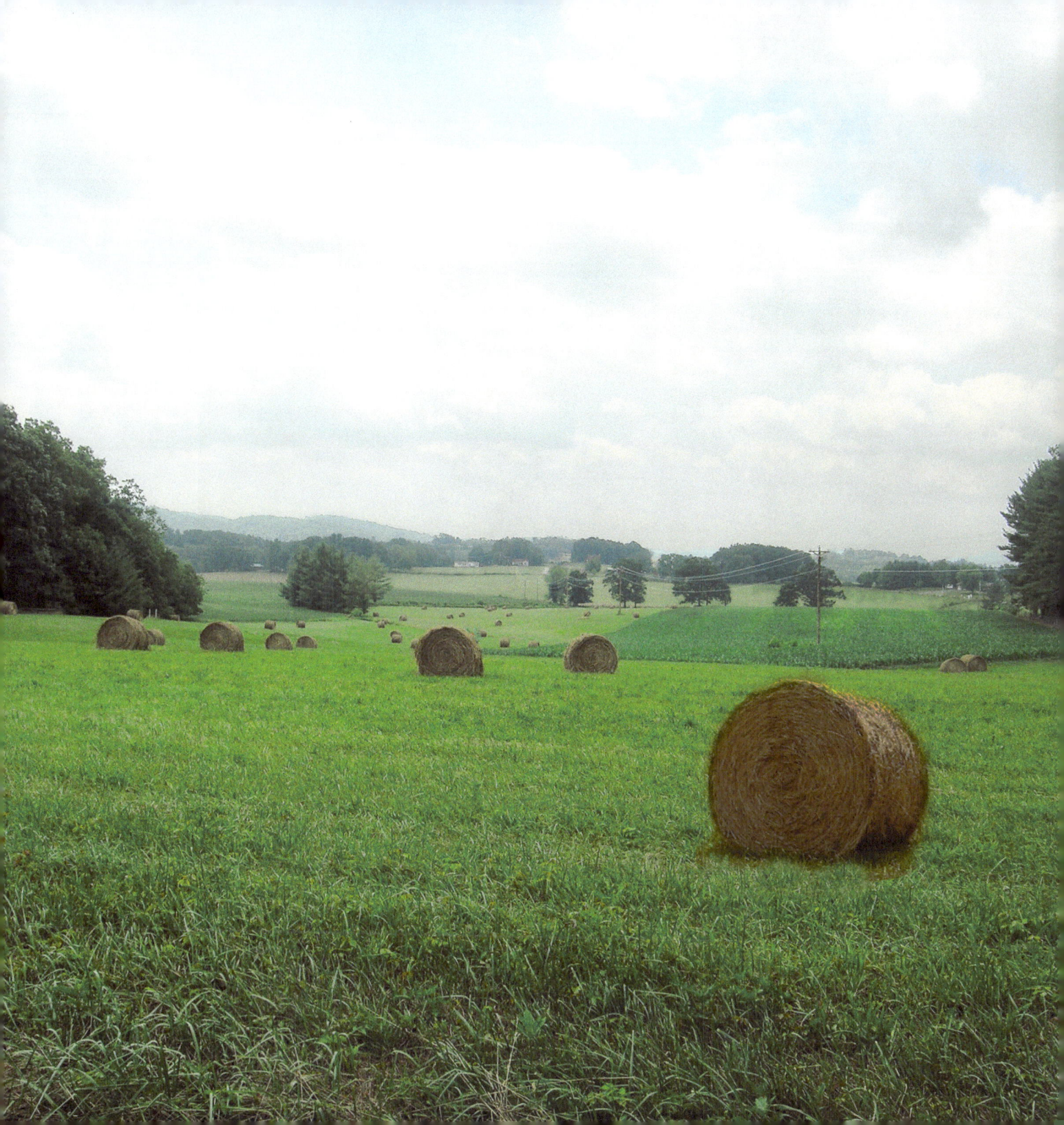

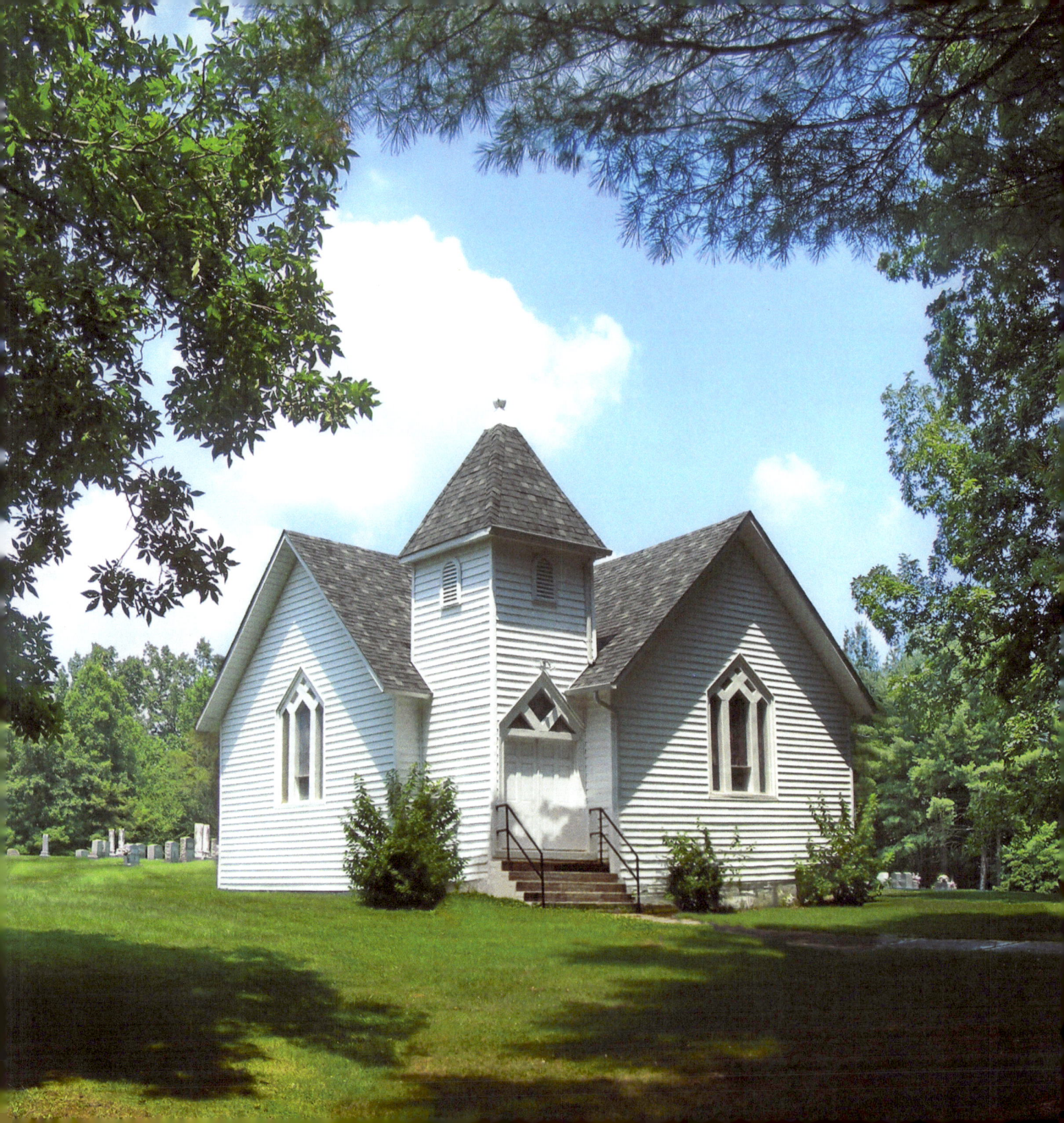

13. **Glade Valley Presbyterian Church**.
The church was established in 1908, two years after
Carson Memorial Presbyterian Church in Sparta
(now Sparta Presbyterian) and a year before Orange
Presbytery built Glade Valley School just up the
road.

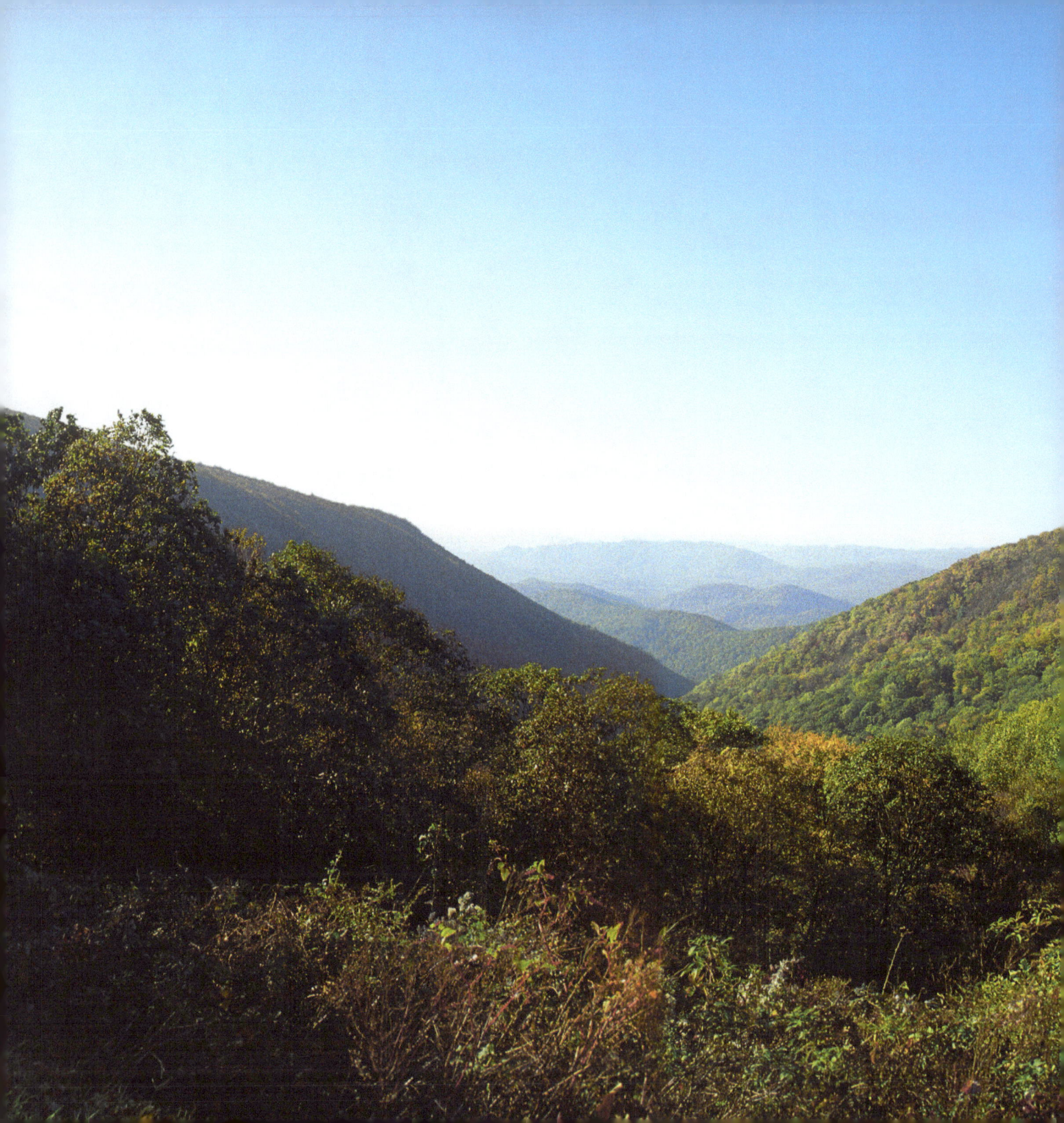

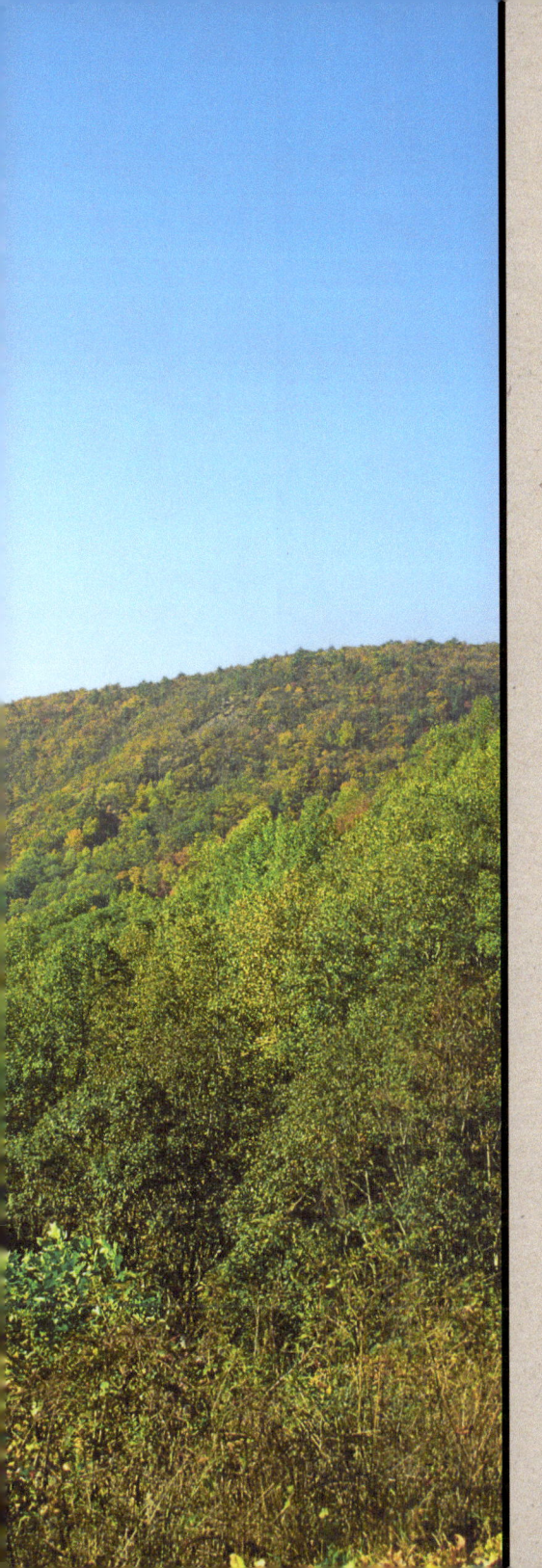

14. **Devils Garden**.
View from the Blue Ridge
Parkway. Named so for either
the snakes in the valley below,
the rocky outcrops in the area or
the pure and spiteful jealousy of
man.

15. **Blueberry Patch**.
Old Orchard Creek Farm
in Lansing, North Carolina,
set ablaze in yearly tradition.
(Following pages)

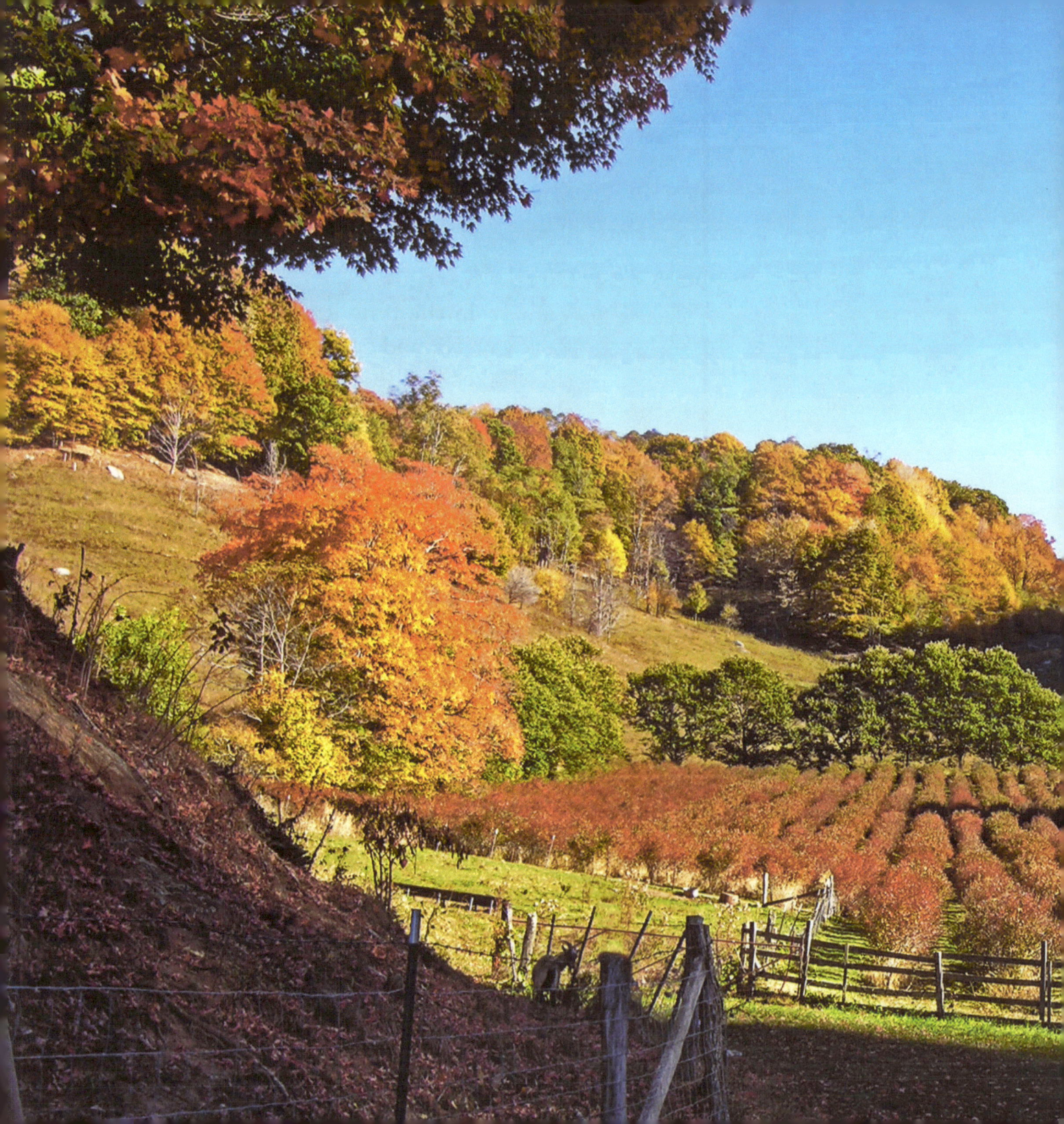

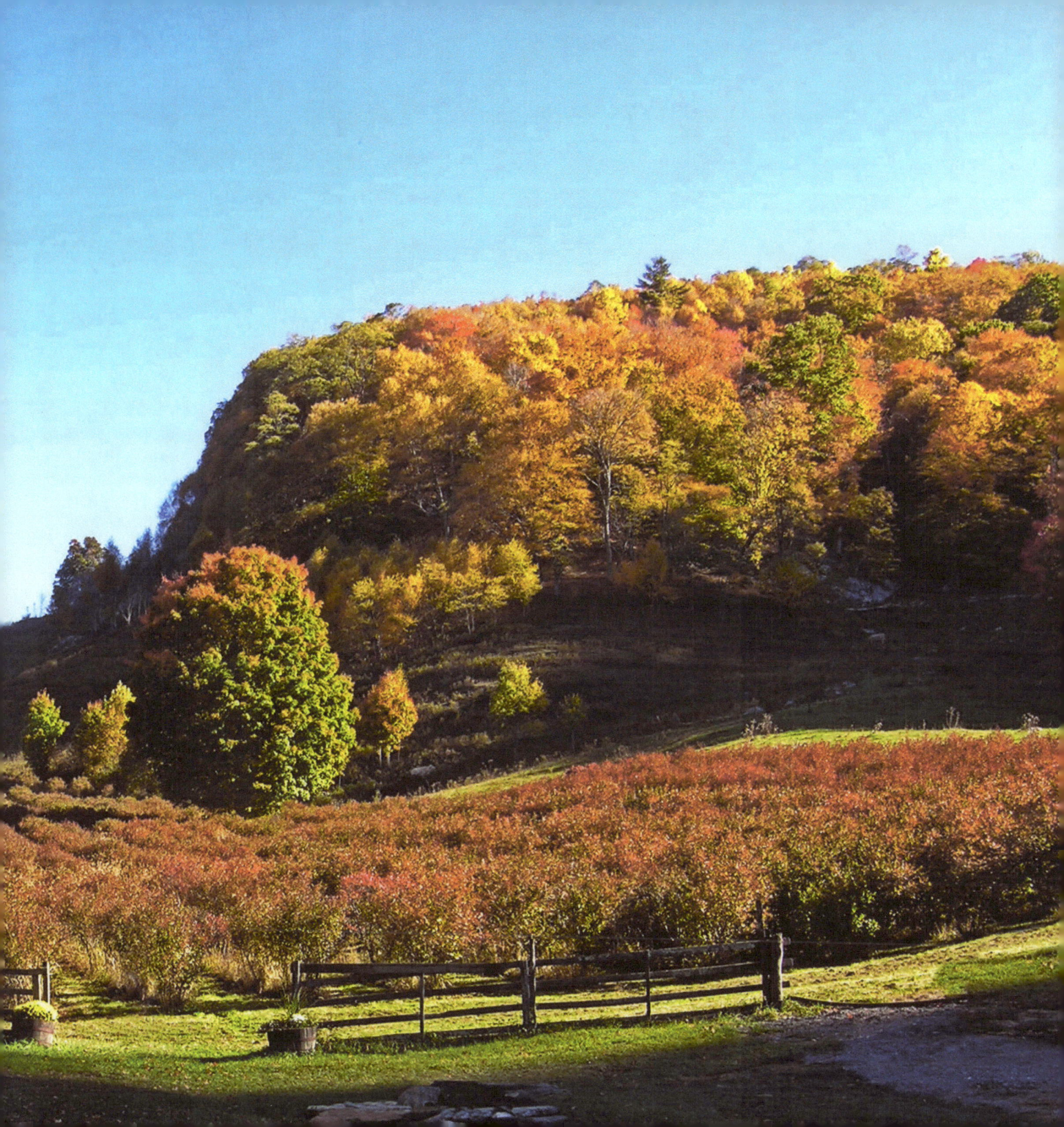

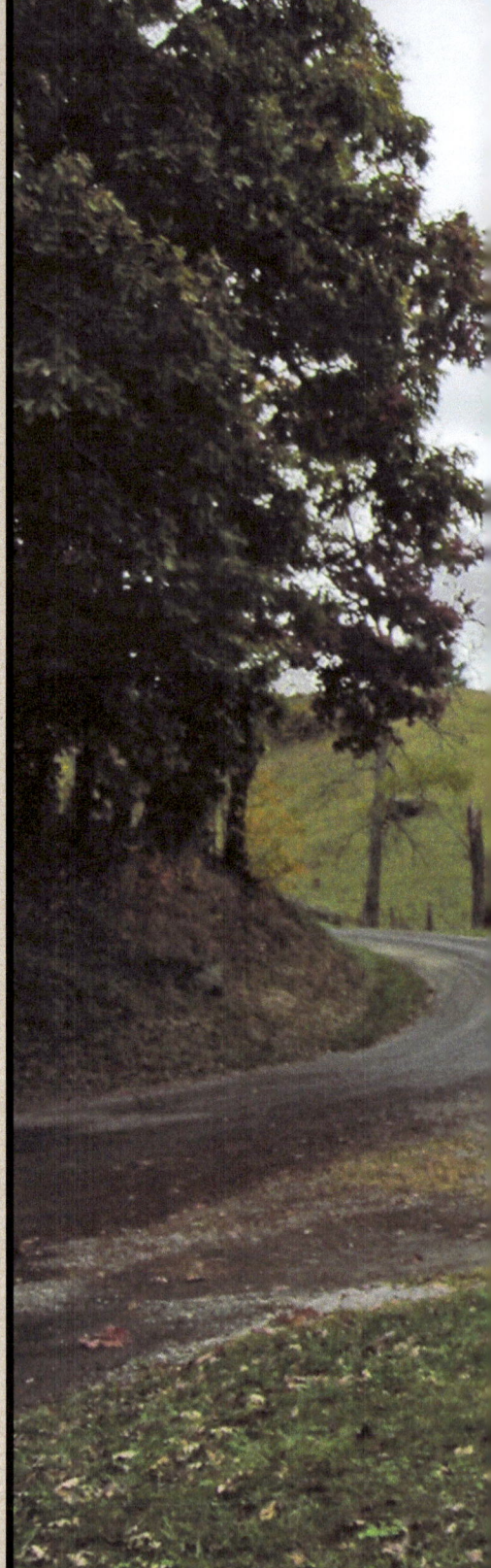

16. **Brush Creek Hall.**
Home of the Highland
Camerata and former home of
Brush Creek Baptist Church,
the building is two miles south
of Independence, Virginia, and
about a mile north of the New
River.

17. **View at Raccoon Holler**.
The comfortable and beautiful
mountain retreat of an old
and venerable, typical
Southern family.
(Following pages)

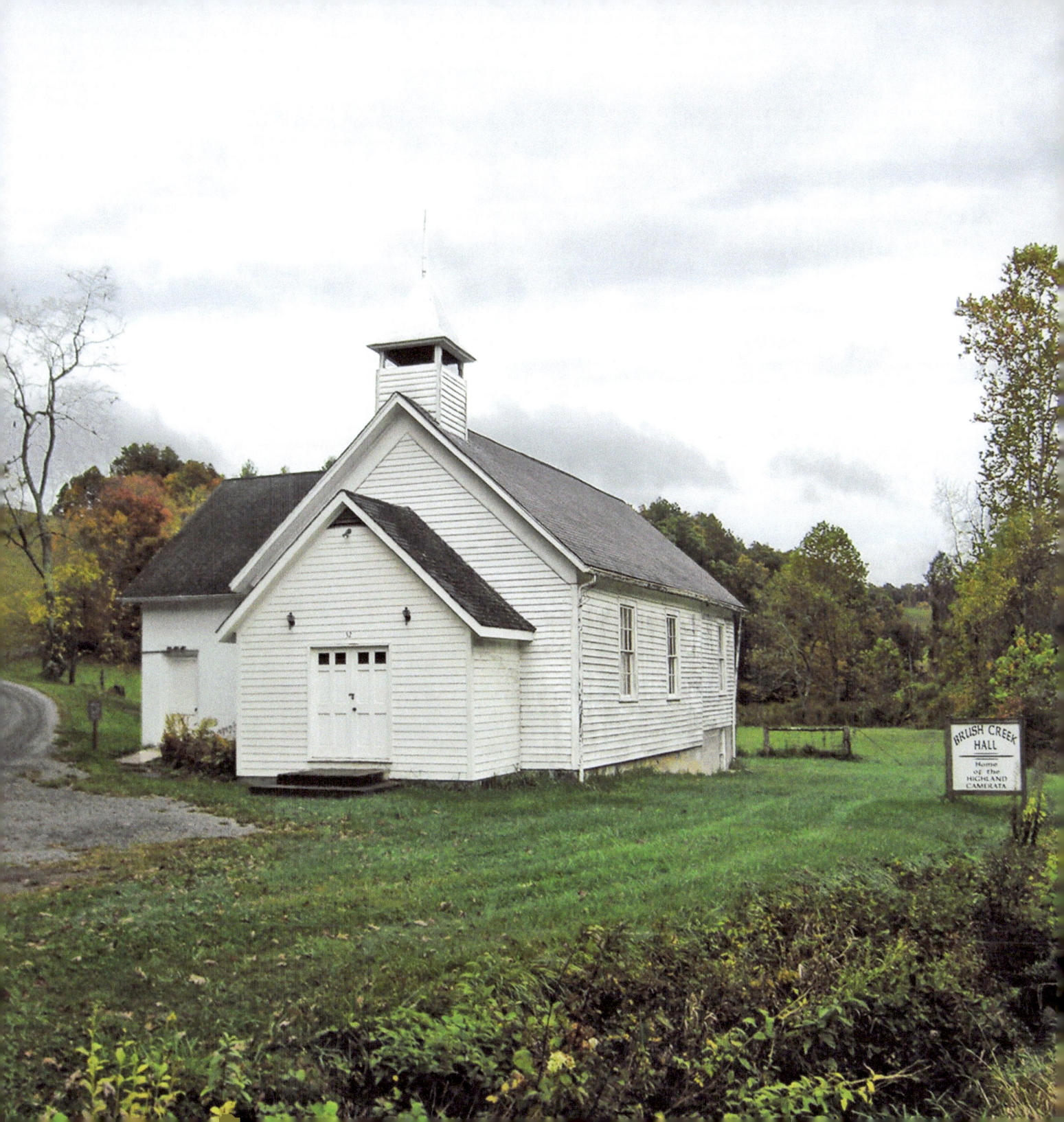

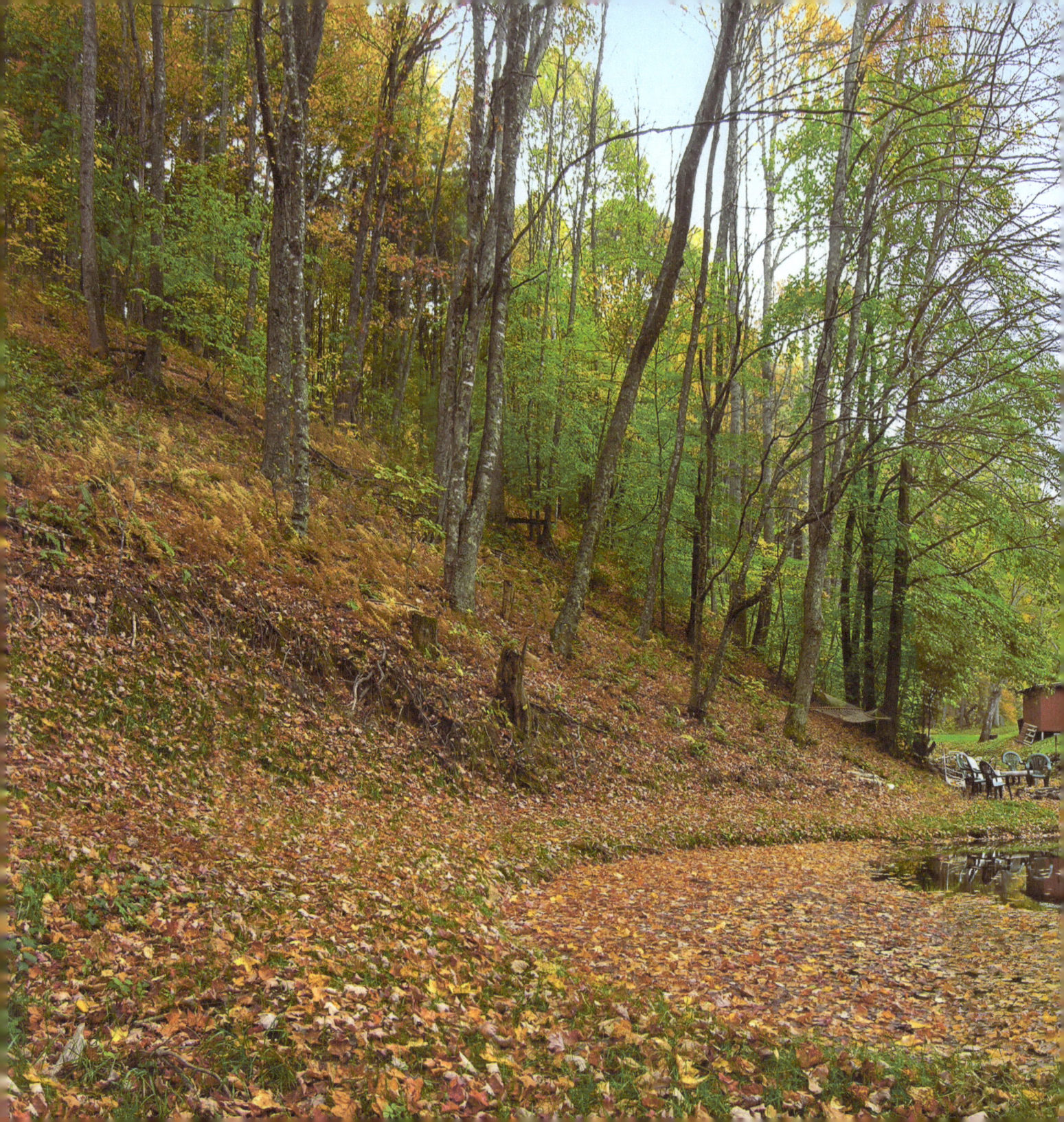

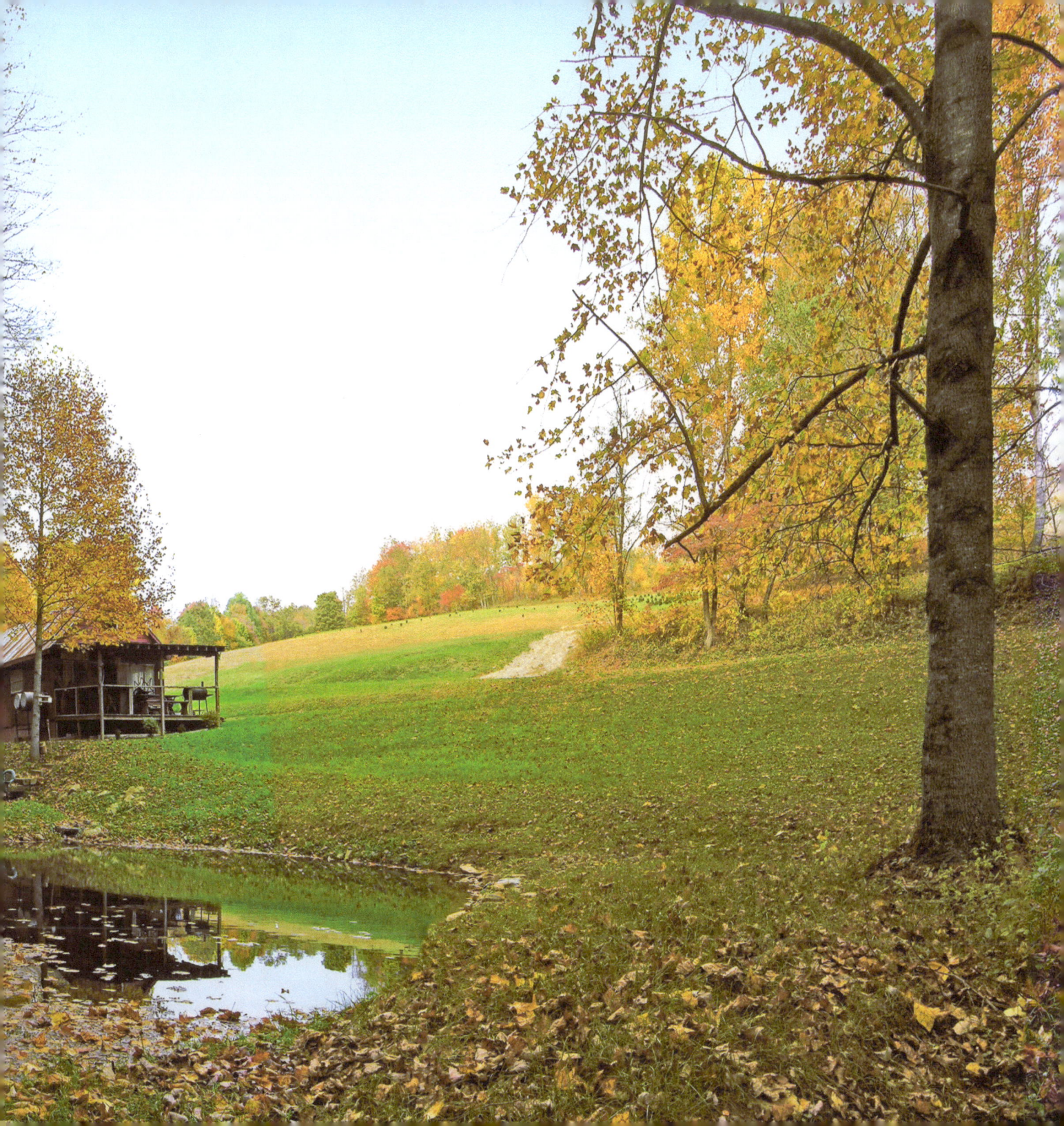

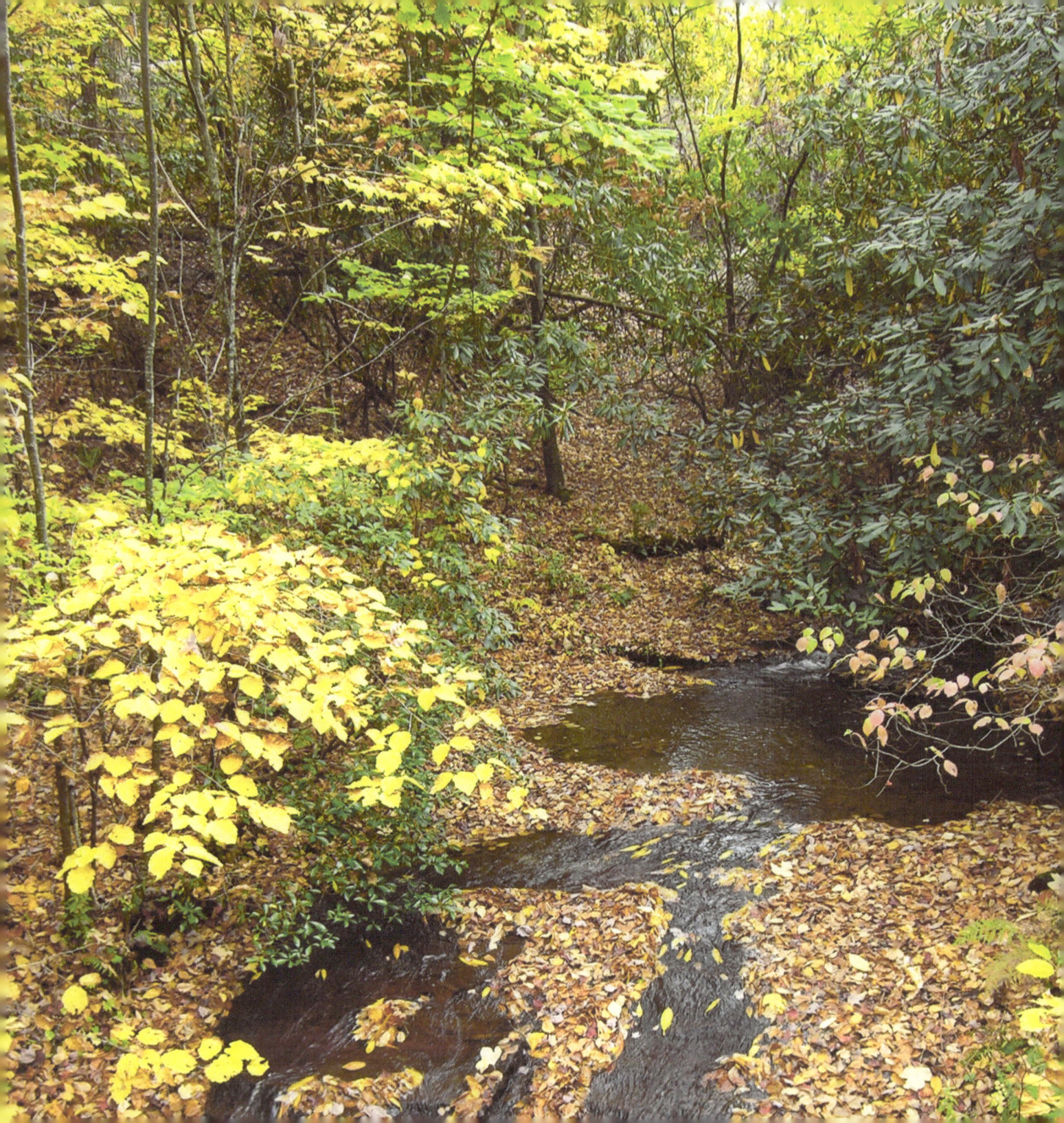

18. **Leafy Cheek Mountain Creek**.
    Sometimes it's nice to think we're
    looking at the same scene the
    Cherokee saw 20 grandfathers ago.

19. **Autumn Earth and Sky**
    violently competing for attention.
    (Following pages)

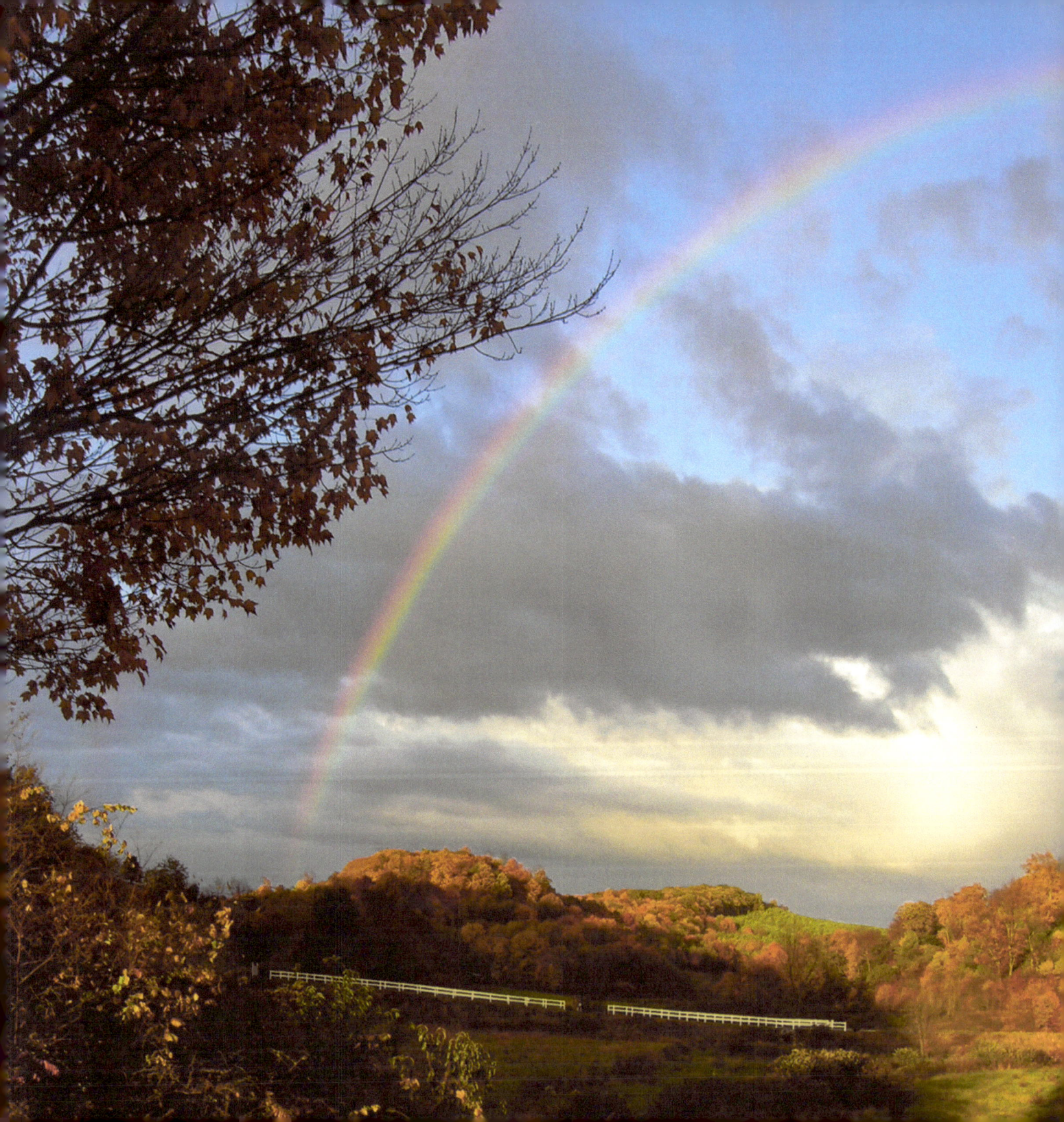

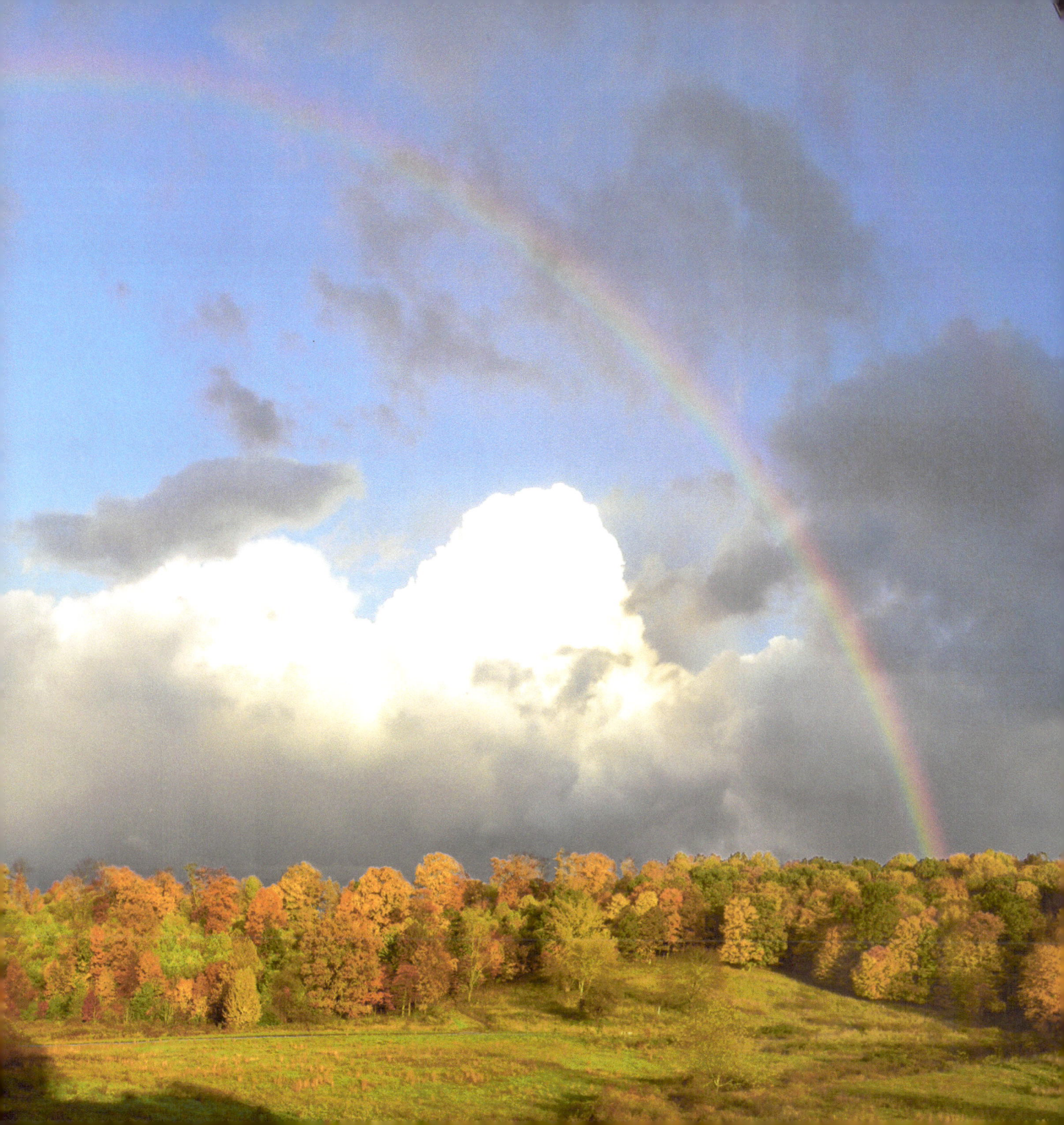

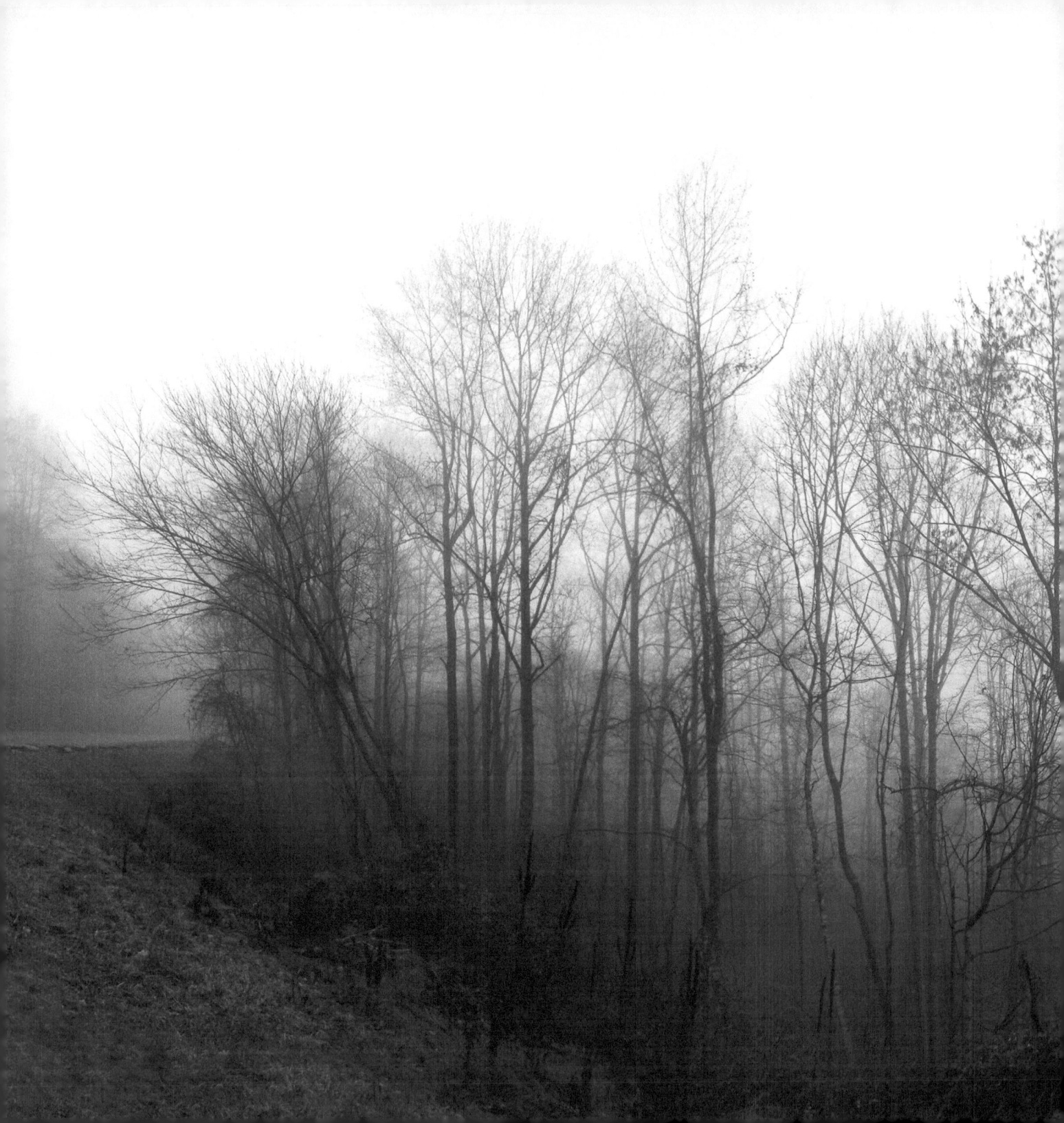

20. **Mountain Mist**.
Silent sentinels,
standing guard.

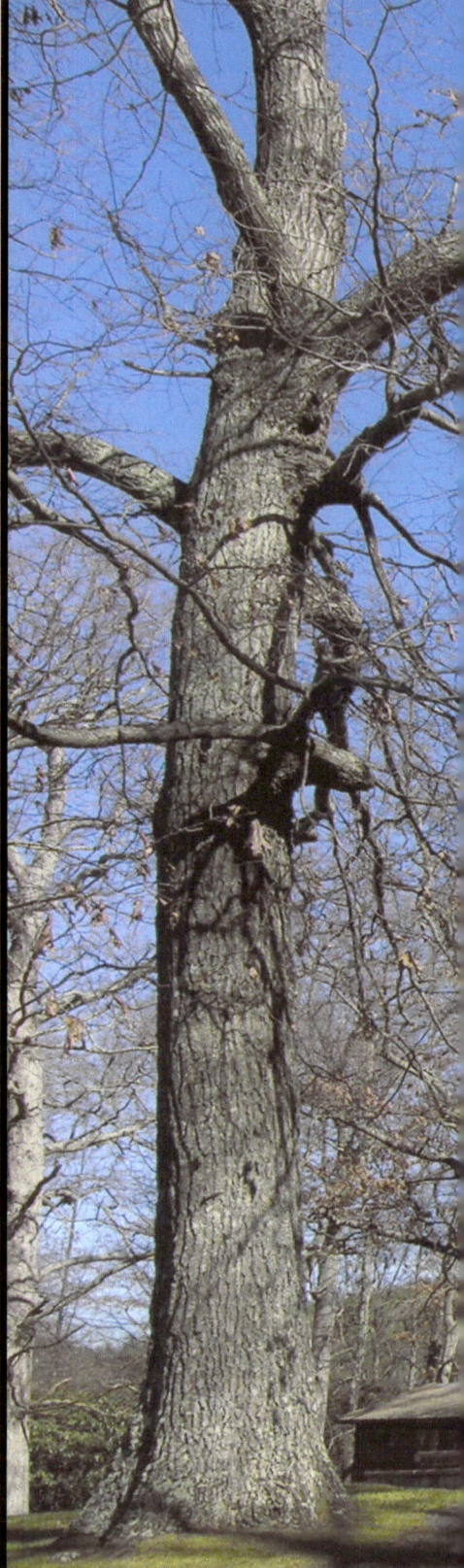

21. **Liberty Missionary
Baptist Church.**
Whitehead, North Carolina.

22. **Chilly Hill**
at Sparta. The bad part
is getting there.
Or leaving there.
(Following pages)

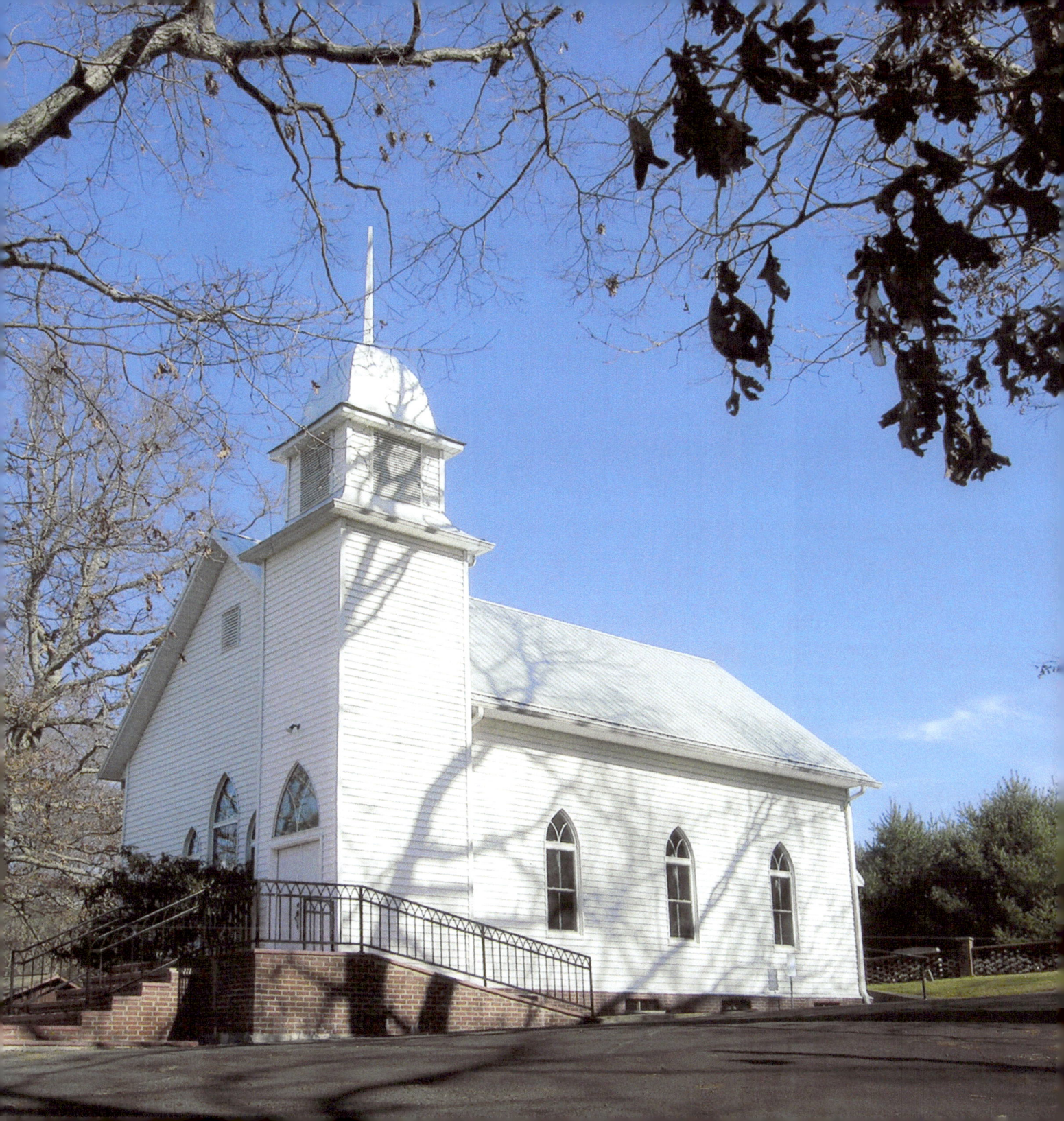

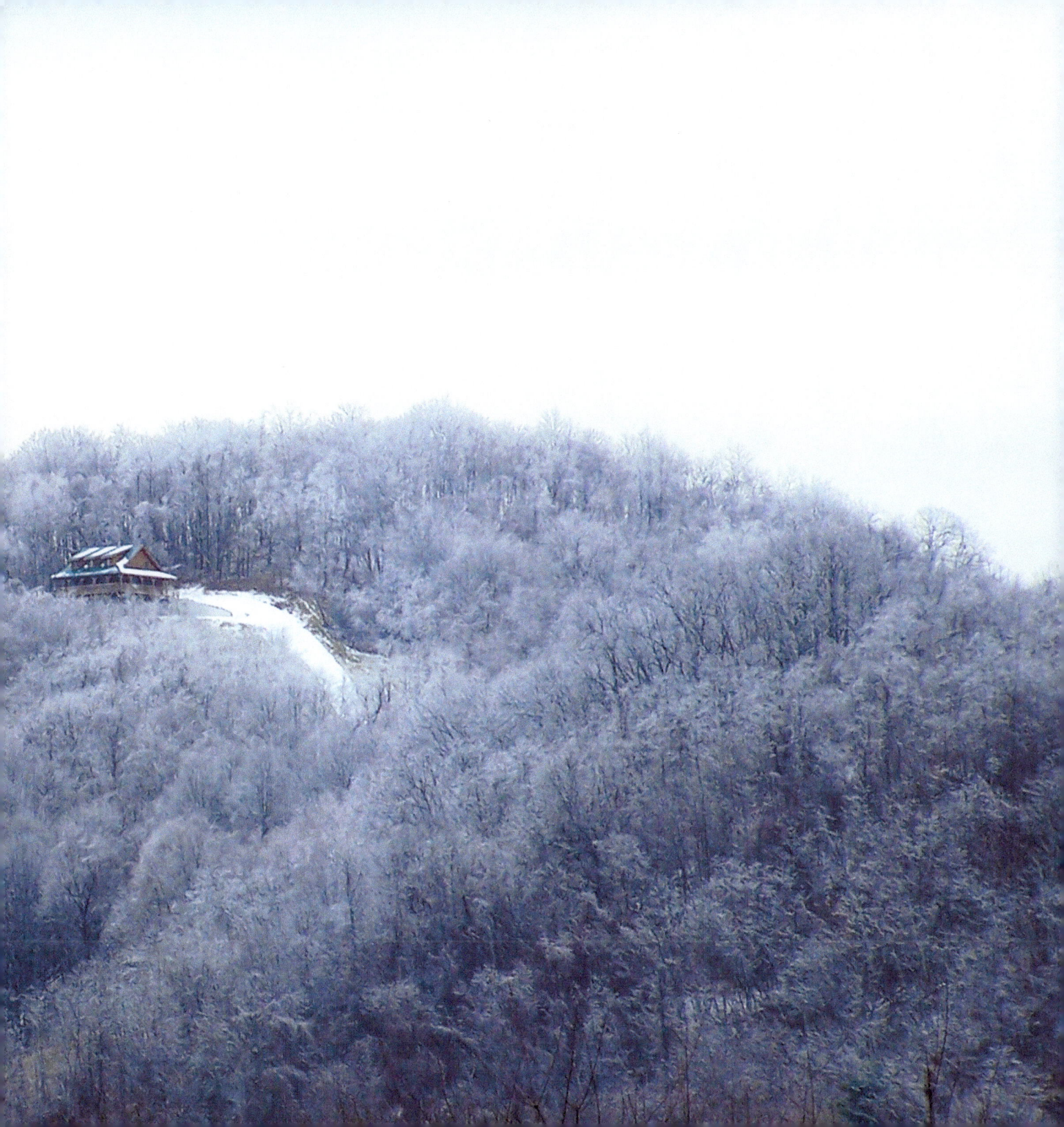

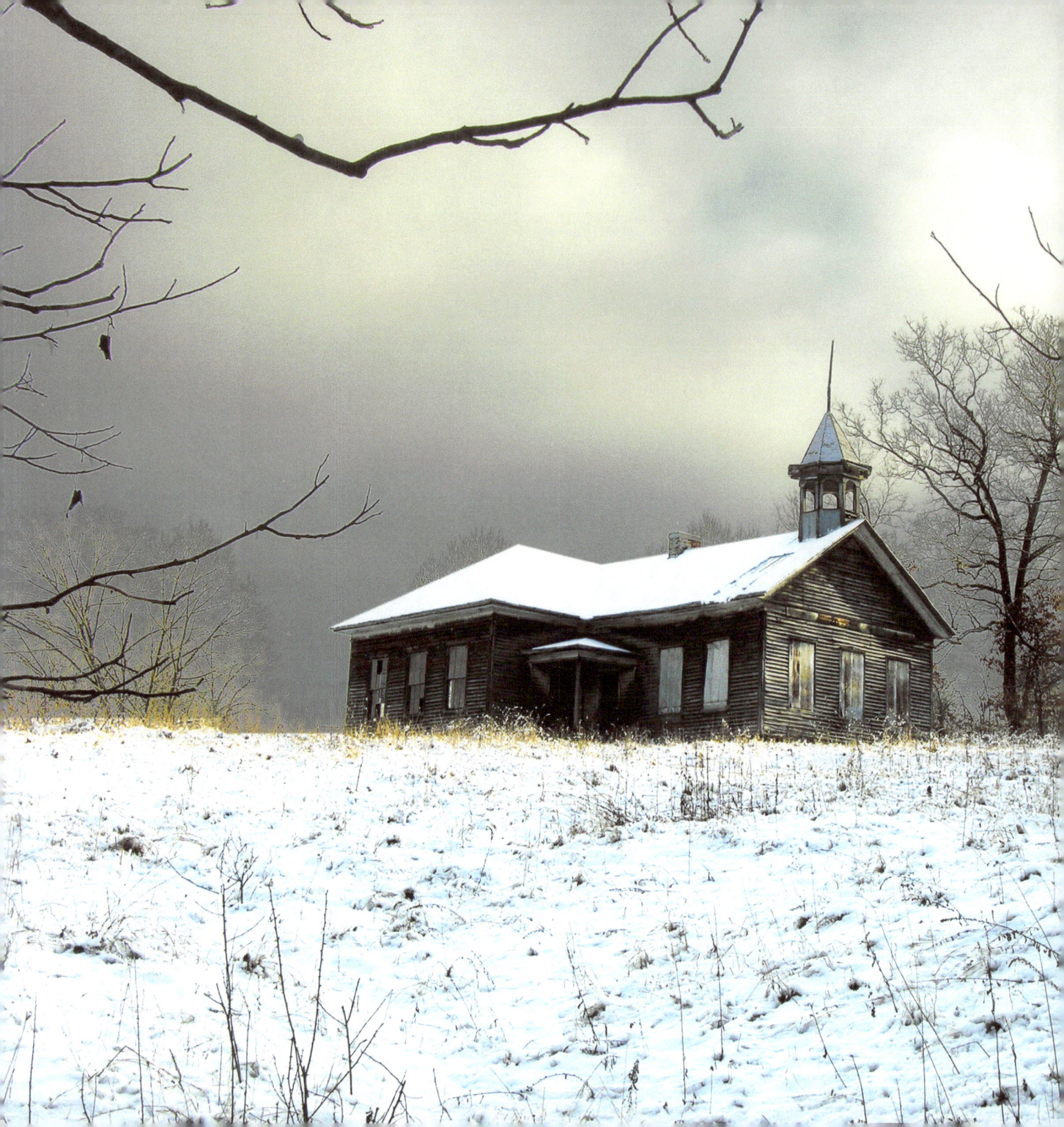

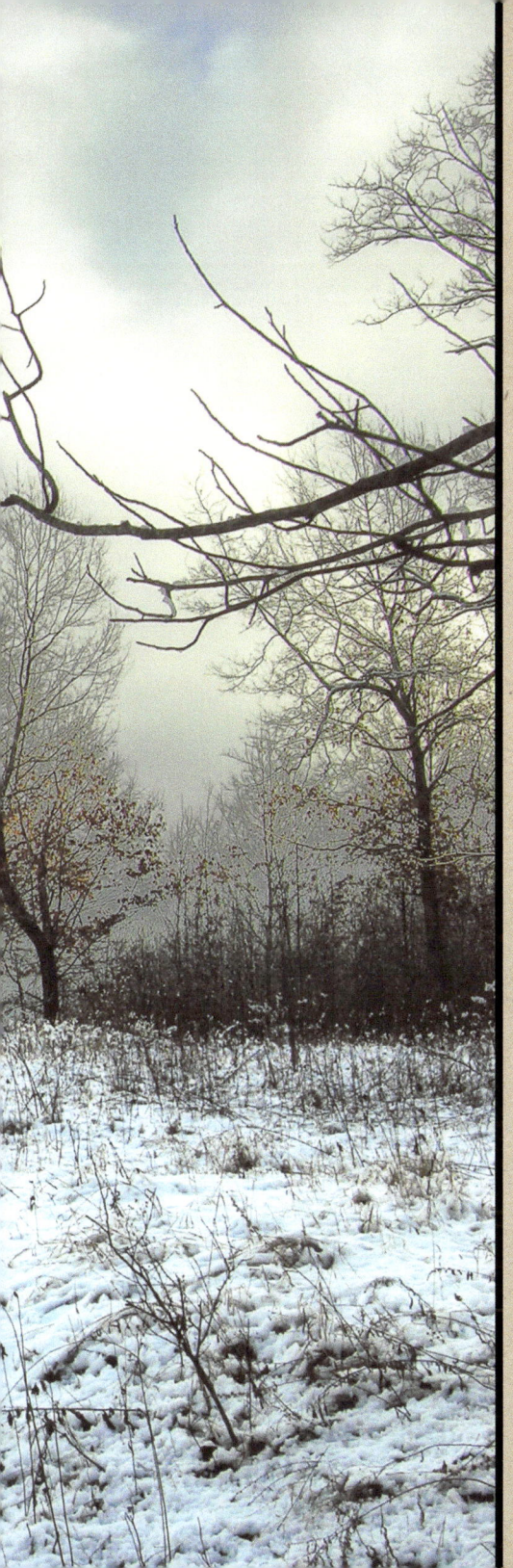

23. **Elk Creek Academy** at Stratford.
Solemn as a cemetery-
surrounded, now, by elderly hills
that once echoed running
feet, squeals and
school bell
peals.

24. **Of Church and State**.

    In absolute defiance,
      of ordinary science,
      (the state debates this news).
    Expert in things empirical,
      they've made a Christmas miracle-
      White lights in colored hues.

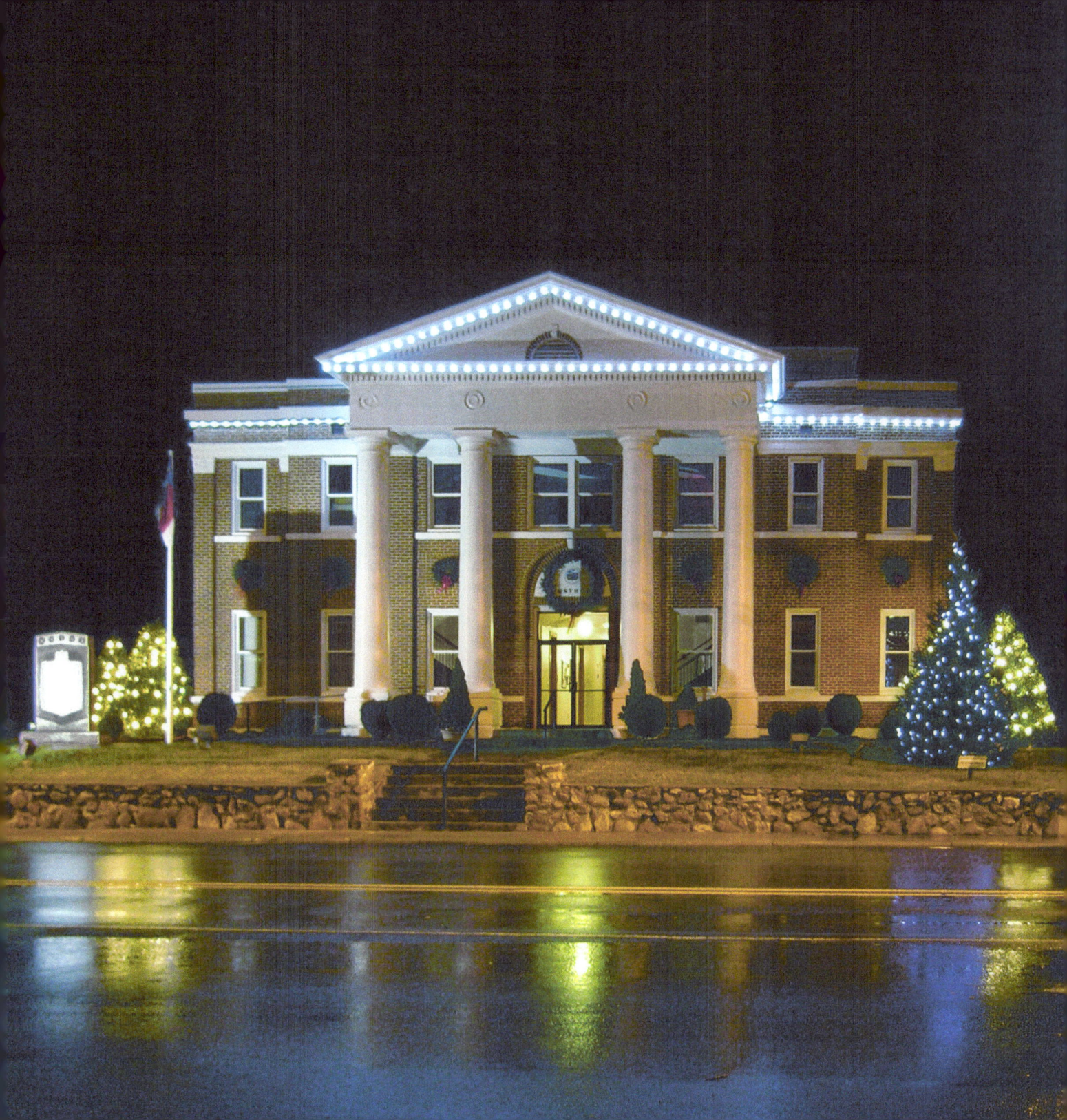

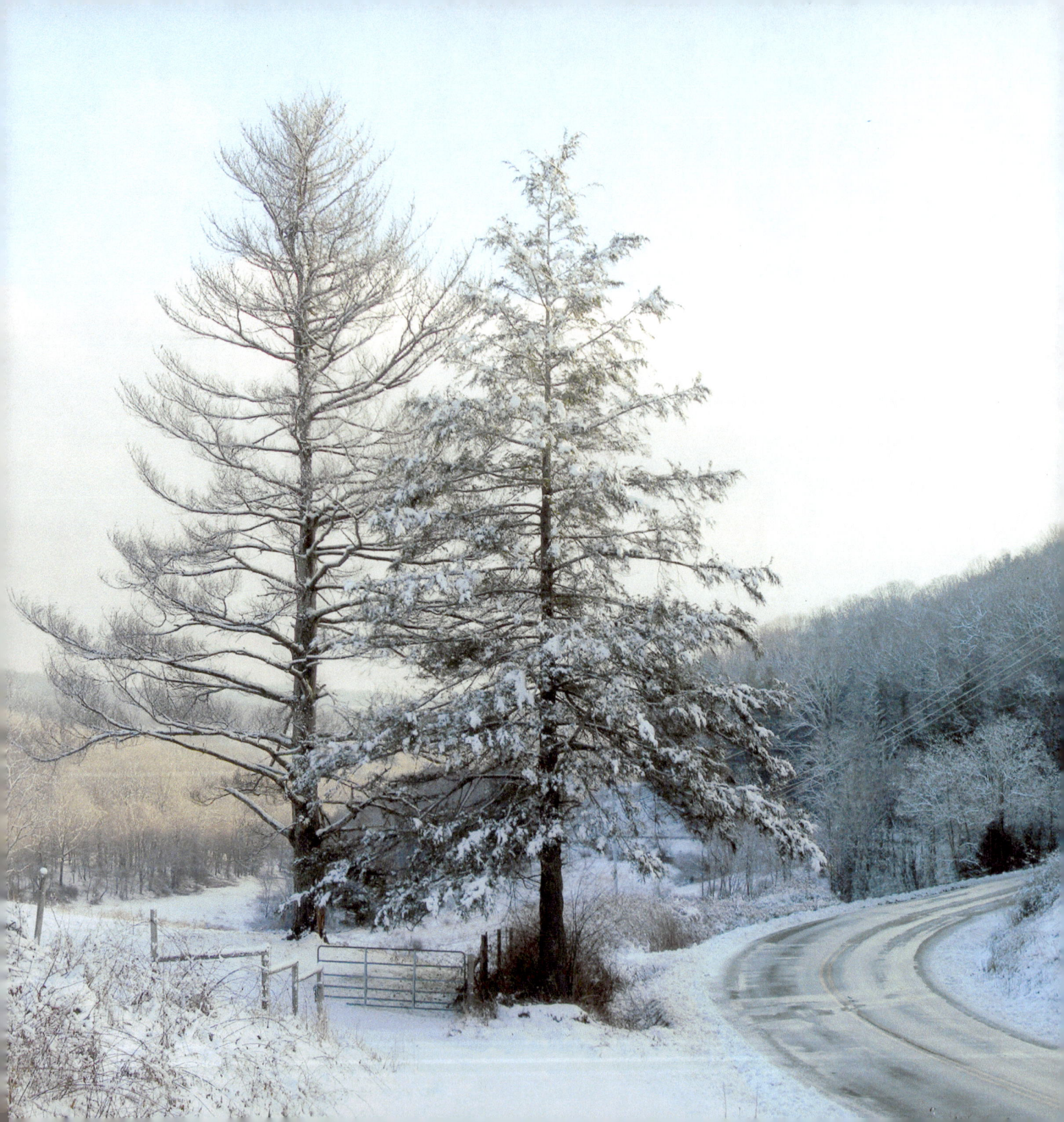

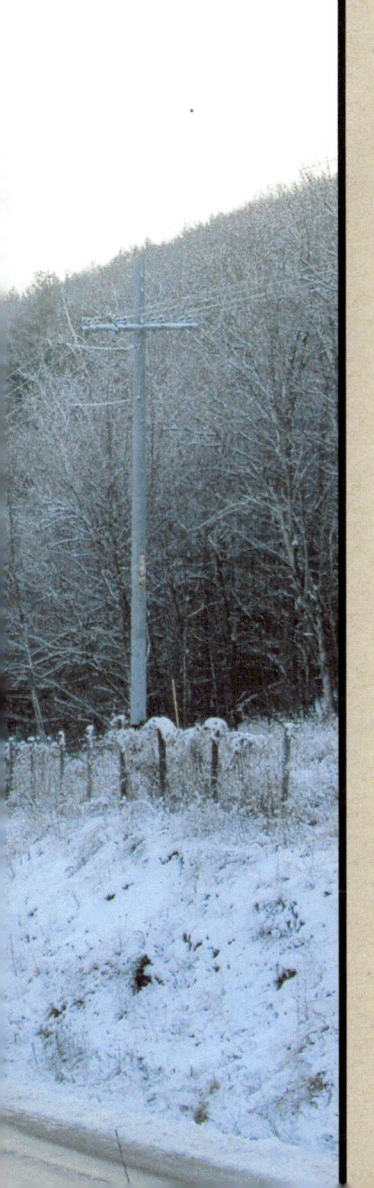

25. **Two Trees** in a cool, blue shade at New Hope.

26. **Chromatic Study in Mono**.
One of my most and least favorite color photographs- for the same reason- lack of color.
(Following pages)

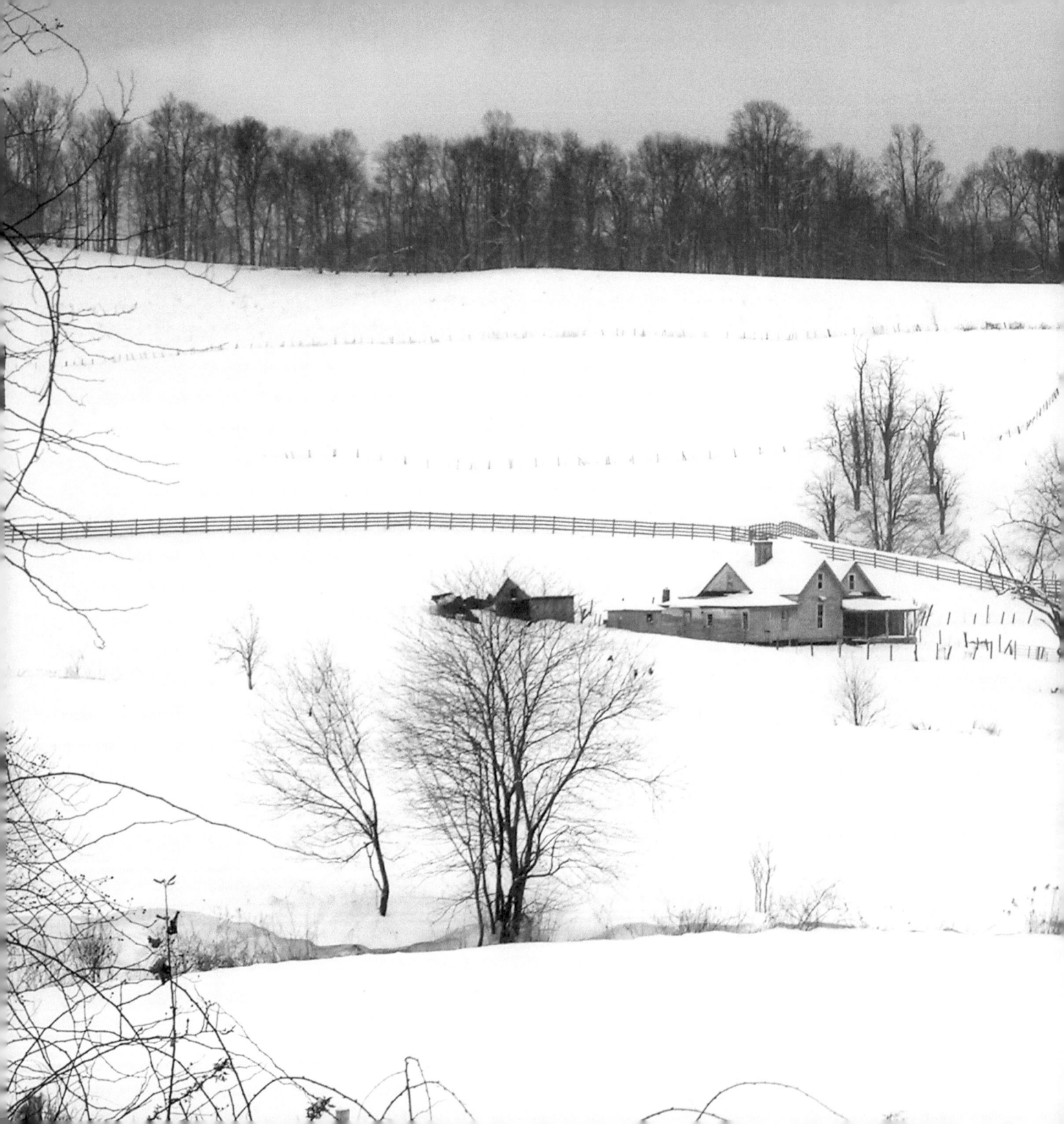

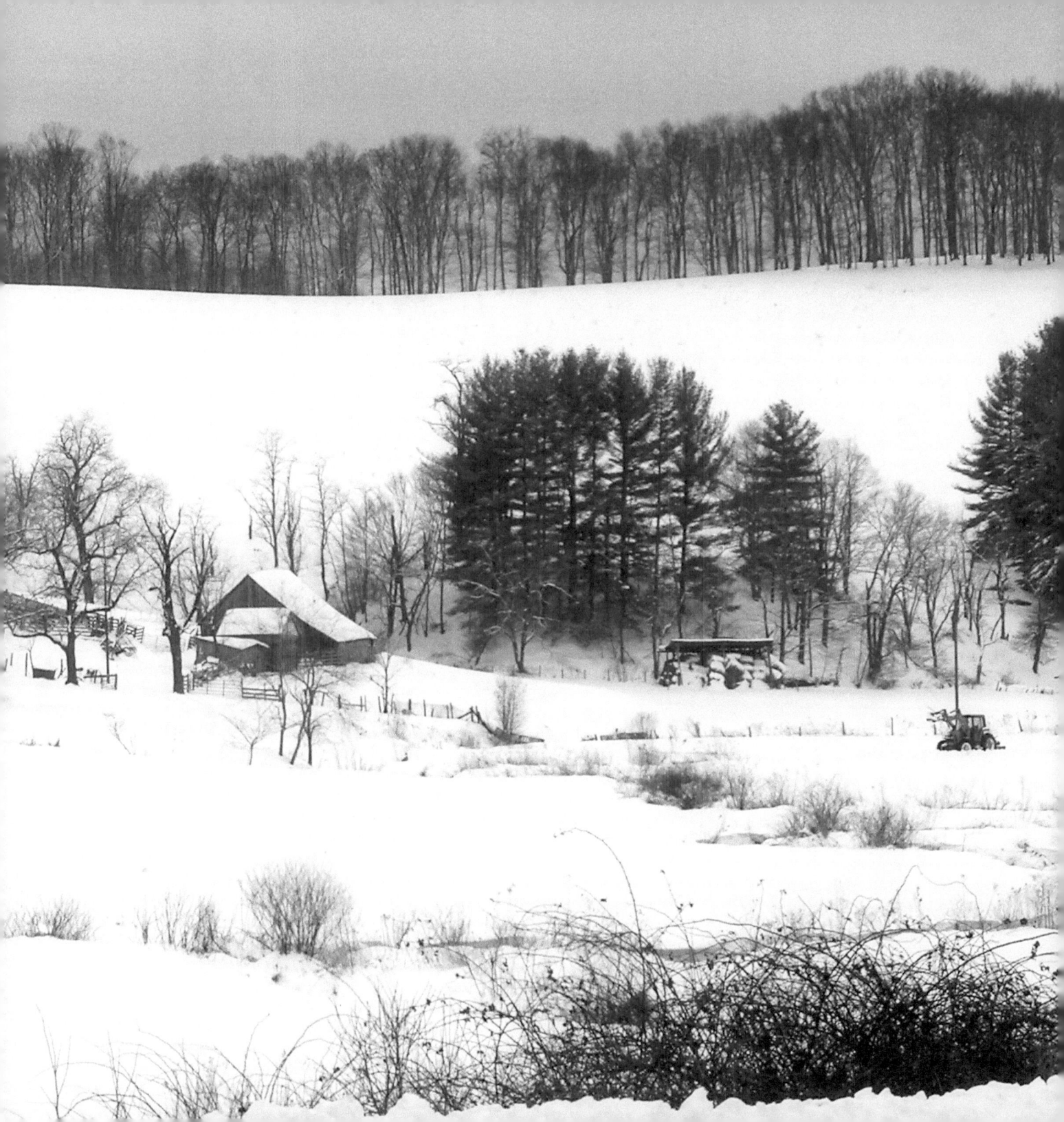

27. **Piney Creek UMC.**
In all its Christmas finery
for yule and times divinery.

28. **Snowy Spruces** shade the way at
Scottville.
(Following pages)

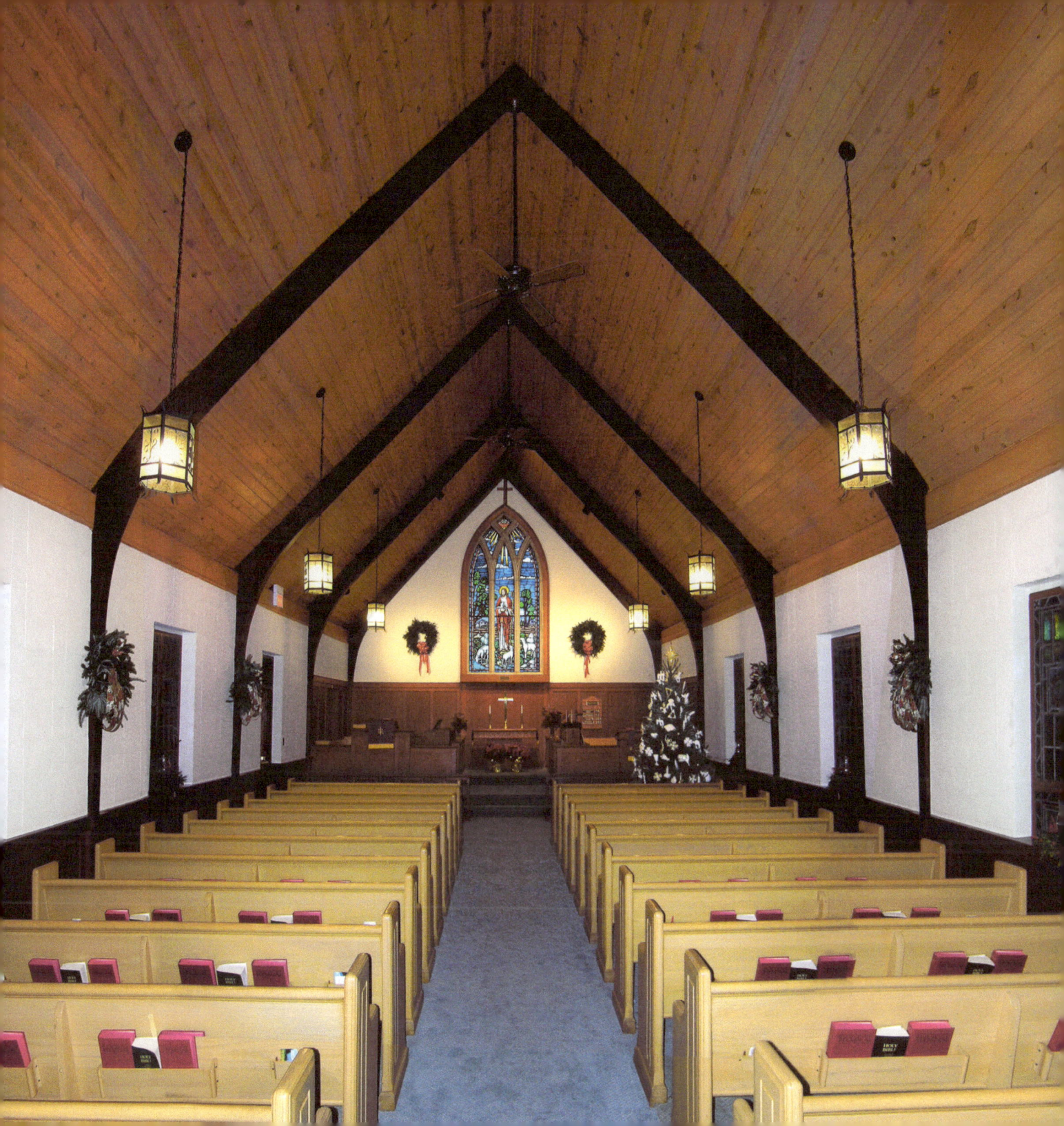

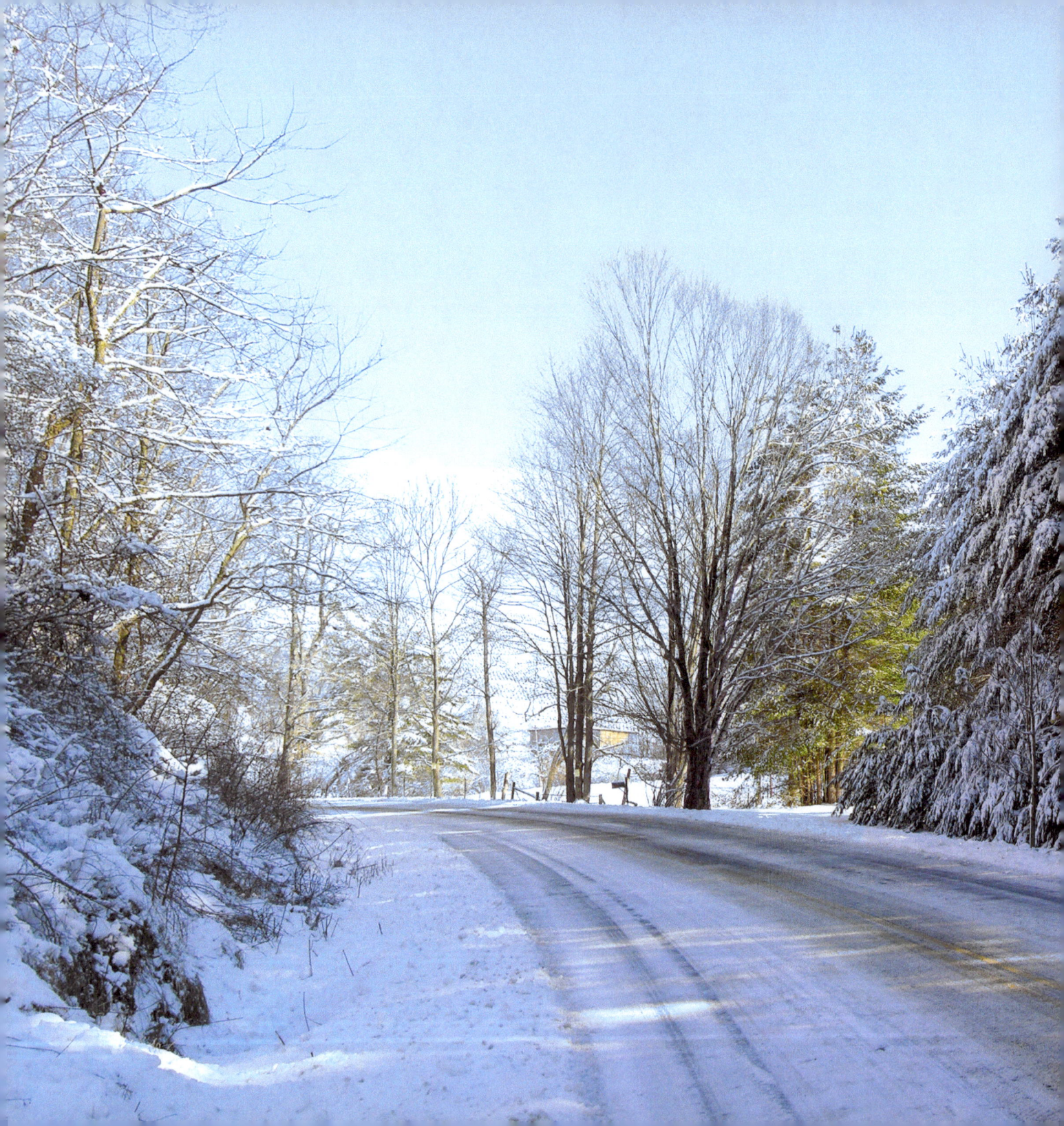

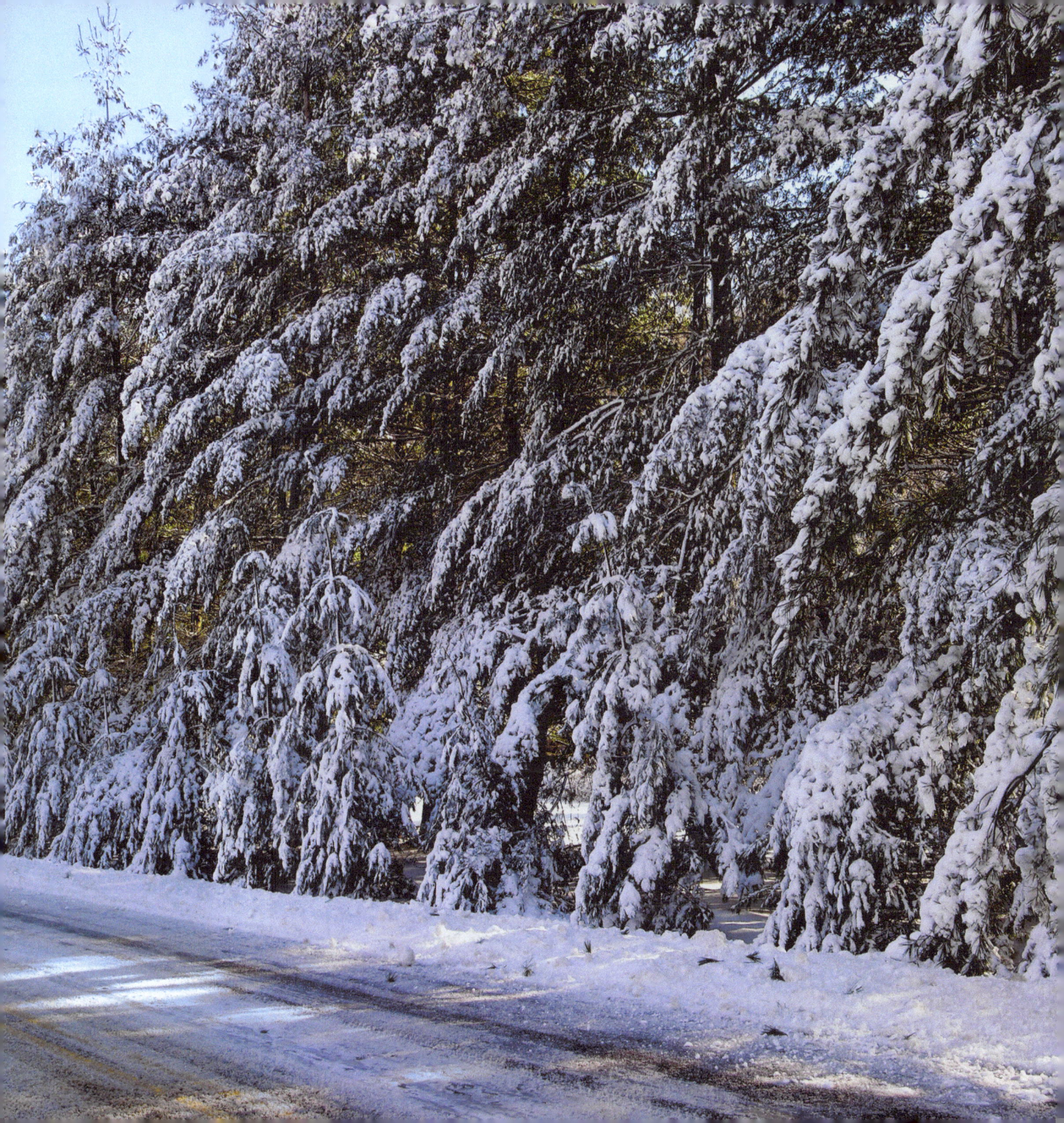

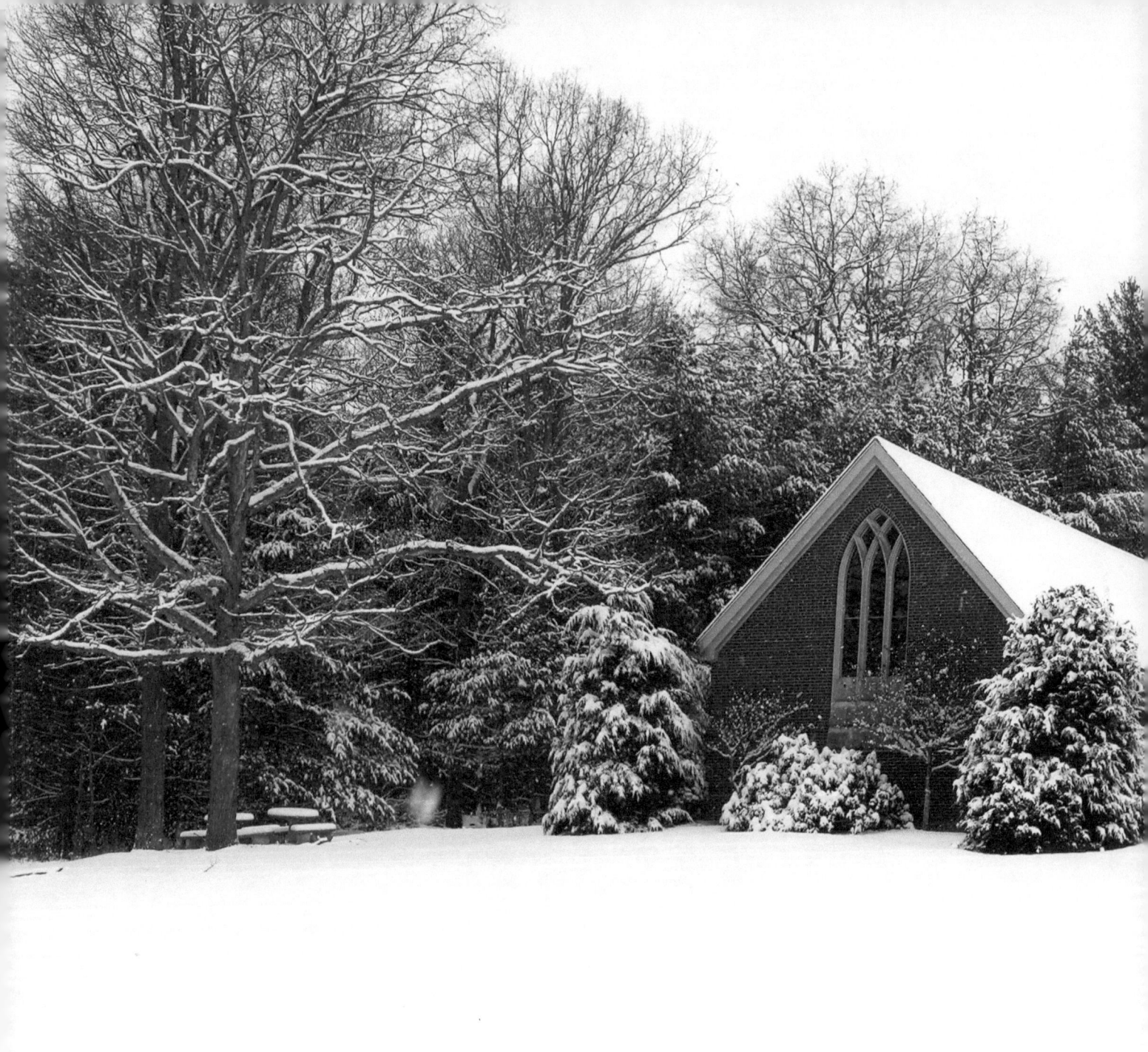

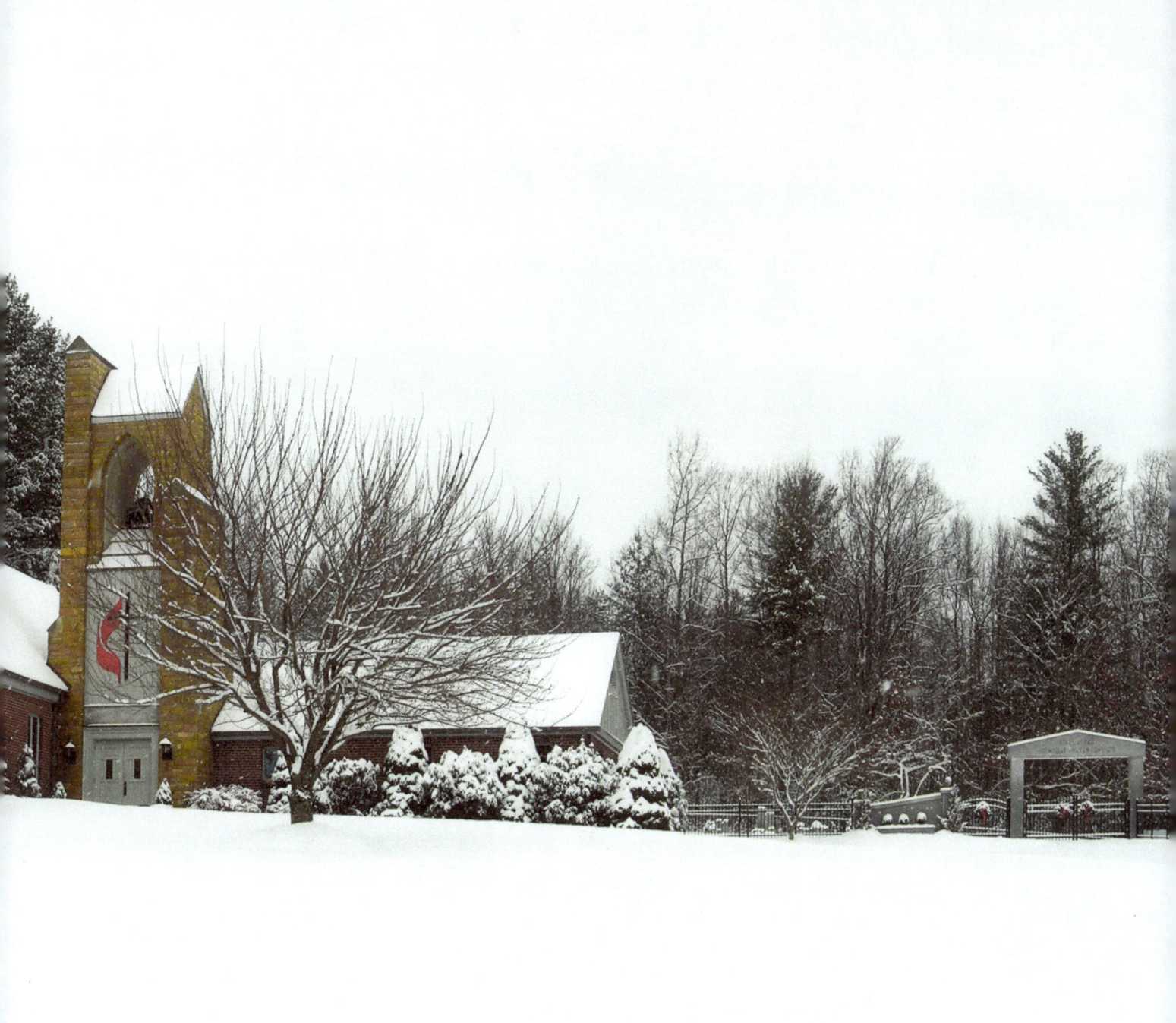

29. **Wintry Churchyard** at Piney Creek.
(Preceding pages)

30. **Lace Vignette** at New Hope.

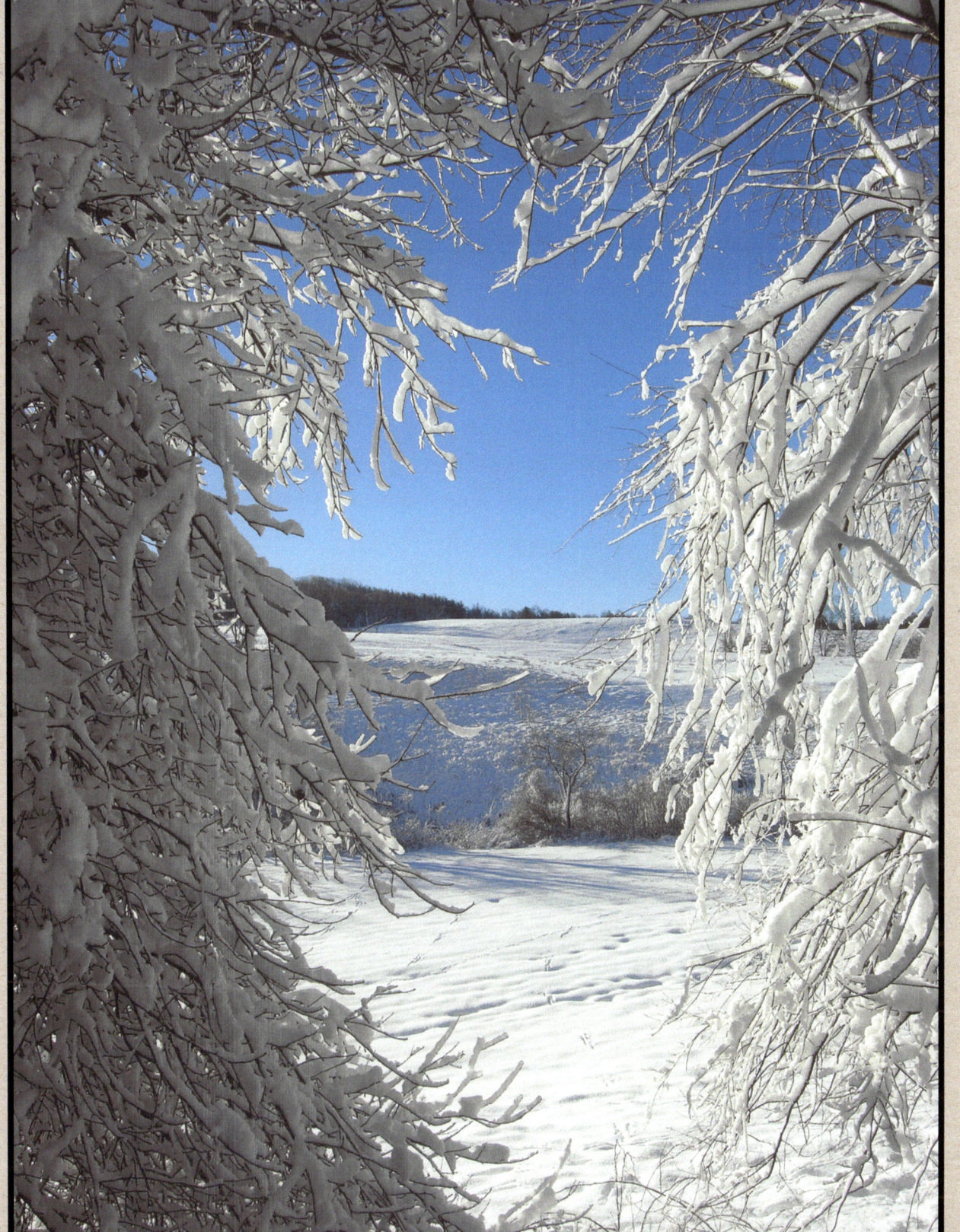

Note

The photography in this series was shot in northwest North Carolina and Southwest Virginia and includes images from film and digital formats. Some were made from multiple exposures, stitched together manually in Adobe® Photoshop.

Some images are part of larger pans and have been cropped to fit this book's format. All photography, editing, page layout and design was done at our shop by Imaging Specialists, Inc. in Sparta, North Carolina.

Martin Brinegar's obituary came from a National Park Service "Historic Resource Study" by Barry M. Buxton.

For more information, please visit:
starroutebooks.com or imagingspecialists.net

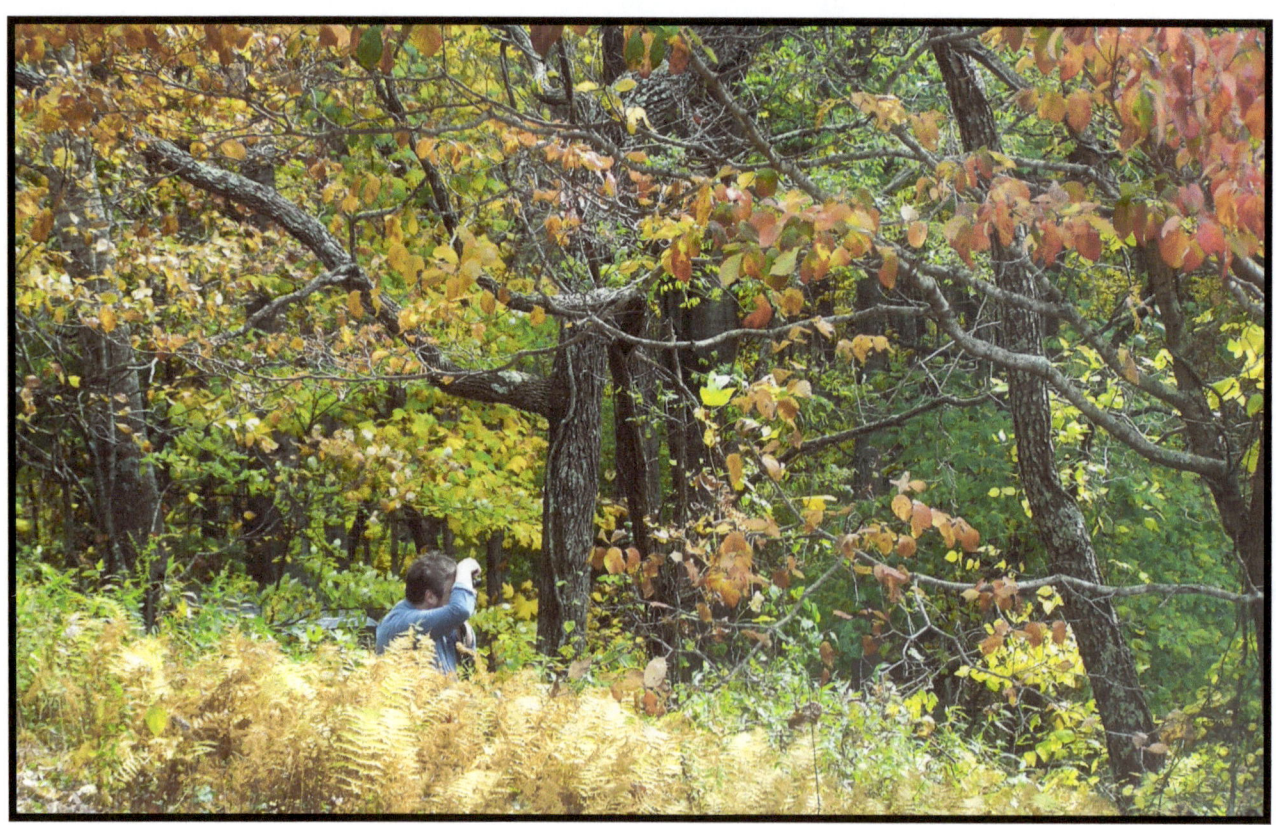

Photo by Claire Halsey